Picture Knits

by Lory Cosgrove

A Sterling/**Lark** Book
Sterling Publishing Co., Inc., New York

Published in paperback 1991 by Sterling Publishing Company, Inc., 387 Park Avenue South, New York, N.Y. 10016

A Sterling / Lark Book

Produced by Altamont Press, Inc., 50 College Street, Asheville, NC 28801

Editor: Dawn Cusick
Design: Rob Pulleyn
Production: Elizabeth Albrecht
Typesetting: Diana Deakin
Photographer: Evan A. Bracken
Technical Assistance: Mary A. Marvel

Library of Congress Cataloging-in-Publication Data

Cosgrove, Lory
Picture knits / by Lory Cosgrove
p.   cm.
"A Sterling/Lark book"
Bibliography: P.
Includes index.
ISBN 0-8069-5756-5
1. Knitting—Patterns   2. Knitting, Machine—Patterns.   3. Sweaters   I. Title
TT825.C712   1989
746.9'2—dc 19   89-31162   CIP

ISBN 0-8069-5756-5 Trade
      0-8069-5757-3 Paper

Distributed in Canada by Sterling Publishing, % Canadian Manda Group, P.O. Box 920, Station U, Toronto, Ontario, Canada M8Z 5P9. Distributed in Great Britain and Europe by Cassell PLC, Villiers House, 41/47 Strand, London WC2N 5JE, England. Distributed in Australia by Capricorn Ltd., P.O. Box 665, Lane Cove, NSW 2066

For Jack & Dolly and all the Cosgrove clan and for TAW.

"But now abide faith, hope, love, these three; but the greatest of these is love." I. Cor. 13:13

ACKNOWLEDGEMENTS
I would like to thank the following people for their help and support in the development of this book: My publisher, Rob Pulleyn of Altamont Press, who helped me develop the theme and direction of this book. Julia Carmichiel, of Excelsior Needleworks, Excelsior, MN., for her encouragement, good humor, and endless supply of hand-knitting knowledge. Terry Gale of Wickham Farm Knitting, Mound, MN., who taught me how to use the knitting machine, and who is always available for help and advice. Susie Mogan, who helped me buy my first knitting machine, and who has always been my best friend. Patty Worthing, Jean Fitzimmons and Cynthia Dunaway, for their lessons in sewing and garment construction. Bob & Ellis Naegele, Norma Robinson, and the BFI Knitters & Quilters (Cathy Robinson, Terre Van Haren, Bear Husom, Jeff Oishi, Kimberly Robie, Jeannie Gockley and Joanne Christ) for their enthusiastic support. And Rocky Olsen for his dust cover photograph.

Yarn Companies
(Mayflower Cotton Helarsgarn)
Neveda Yarn Company
80 13 Avenue
Ronkonkoma, NY 11779

(Germantown)
Brunswick Worsted Mills, Inc.
P.O. Box 276
Pickens, SC 29671

Illustrations Page 18
Used by permission of the
Knitking Corporation

Knitting Machine Companies
Brother Knitting Machines
8 Corporate Place
Piscataway, NJ 08854

Machine Knitting Consultant
Terry Gale
Wickham Farm Knitting
7210 Co. Rd. 110 West
Mound, MN 55364

Knitking Corporation
1128 Crenshaw Blvd.
Los Angeles, CA

Hand Knitting Consultant
Julia Carmichiel
Excelsior Needleworks, Ltd.
432 2nd Street
Excelsior, MN 55331

Technical Consultant
Nola Theiss
Neveda Yarn Company
Ronkonkoma, NY 11779

Table of Contents

Introduction

When I was a little girl, I inherited a reindeer sweater made by my best friend's mother out of sturdy knitting worsted yarn. It was too big for me and I had to roll up the sleeves, but I loved the pretty white reindeer on the lively cardinal-red background. I wore that sweater until I grew out of it, and then it was passed along to each of my eight brothers and sisters until baby Jim, 12 years my junior, finally wore the elbows out of it.

Many happy family memories are tied to that reindeer sweater — raking leaves on crisp, blue October days, skiing and sledding in the clear, cold Minnesota winter, and sitting around the fireplace, stringing popcorn for the Christmas tree.

When I grew up, I learned to knit. My first big project was a navy crew-neck pullover in very cheap yarn. After hours of struggling with incomprehensible directions (" - In the 89th row . . .") and endless unraveling and reworking, I ended up with an unwearable garment, frustration, and a heap of yarn soaked in tears.

I put my needles away, convinced that knitting was not for me. Years later, I stumbled across a pattern for a reindeer sweater and all of my childhood memories came rushing back. I bought some good wool yarn, and with the help and advice of a friend, made a lovely sweater. Truly addicted now, I decided to design my own sweaters so that I wouldn't have to make the same pattern over and over again.

I love working in two or more colors because the contrasting colors do most of the row counting for you (e.g. you only need to count 4 rows between each row of dots.) Also, it's fun to see the patterns emerge from your work as you go along, and there are no complicated stitches — just knit and purl.

Each of the 40 sweaters in this book is shown in a full-page color photo, with instructions for sizes fitting children to large adults.

While experienced knitters will find this book filled with enjoyable projects, I have designed the format with the beginning and intermediate knitter in mind. Anyone who can knit in an even tension can make a picture knit sweater.

Since all of these sweaters can also be made on a good bulky knitting machine, I have included a chapter of machine-knitting tips —all those things they don't give you instructions for when you buy the machine. I spent over a month working the same piece over and over on my machine until I got just what I wanted. I am happy to share these tips with you.

For inspiration, I've also included a wide selection of additional pattern and border design graphs. Mix and match these patterns to create your own unique sweaters. A knitting alphabet for adding names and monograms will personalize your work even more.

I hope you will enjoy makng thse sweaters as much as I have enjoyed designing them.

Lory Cosgrove

4

1.

Hand Knitting

In this chapter you will find tips for hand knitting the sweaters in this book, followed by directions for men's, women's, and children's sizes. Since all of the sweaters are the same basic pattern, the same set of directions is used for every sweater. Only the designs and sizes vary. Think of it this way: the directions will determine the size and shape of your garment, while the picture graphs and the yarn colors you choose will determine the uniqueness of your sweaters. (Directions for the baby bag shown on pages 110 and 113 are on pages 114 - 115.)

You will notice that some sweaters have the picture design across the top of the sweater, while others have the picture design on the bottom half of the sweater (below the underarm decrease). The pattern directions take this factor into account.

Remember that you are working with two elements at the same time. The first is size, which is determined for each section of your garment by width and length. Width is determined by the number of stitches across your needle at the required gauge, and length is measured simply in inches. For the front and back pieces, measure from the beginning of the ribbing up to the start of the top border (**A** to **B**), and from the end of the top border up to the shoulder decrease (**C** to **D**). (See illustration below). In the case of the sleeves, you will only measure from the beginning of the ribbing up to the top border. The sleeve cap decreases naturally.

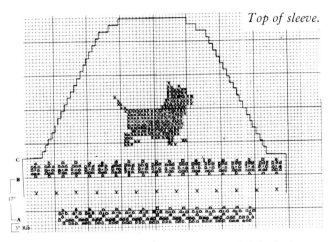

Top of sleeve.

The second element you are working with is design placement. You will always want your picture pattern to be nicely balanced on your sweater. To keep the design balanced, you must remember to add or subtract the same number of stitches from each side of your pattern graph when increasing or decreasing size. The bottom of each graph is marked in increments of ten stitches, with zero at the center of each design.

For example, all the women's sweater pattern graphs are graphed out for a size 34-36 (95 stitches at beginning). So if you want to make the sweater in a 38-40 (99 stitches at beginning), you must add 2 stitches to each side of the graph. An easy way to do this is to mark a pencil line right on the graph on each side of the pattern.

☐ *Knitting in Two or More Colors: The Fairisles Technique*

Although it looks difficult to the uninitiated, knitting in two or more colors is very easy. Once you've mastered the technique, you can knit a wide variety of beautiful garments and even create your own designs. There are no difficult stitches to learn; only the simple knit and purl are used. Because there are usually only a few rows of plain knitting between rows of patterned knitting, you'll never face the boredom of counting endless rows of stitches.

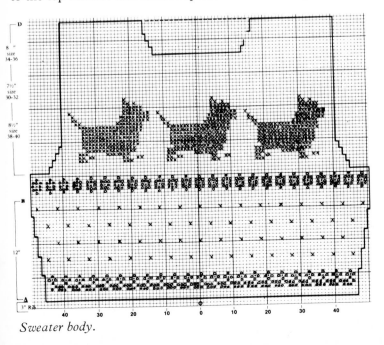

Sweater body.

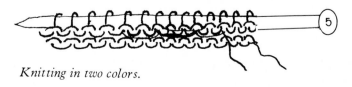

Knitting in two colors.

5

□ Changing From One Color Yarn to Another

Each stitch is made from only one color of yarn. Always start knitting in your background color. This is the color that you will use the greatest amount of for your project. Your secondary color is the yarn used to "paint" the picture of your pattern design. This secondary yarn color is carried along with your background yarn color. Each time your picture pattern graph indicates a stitch in your secondary color, just make that stitch in the second color and carry the background color until you need it again. Do not tie on your second color. Just let the end hang loose until the piece is finished. Your loose yarn is always carried on the purl side of your work, just as in all other knitting projects.

If your project calls for a third color, simply add another strand of yarn to your work. At any given time you'll be knitting in one color while carrying two colors on the wrong side of your work.

□ Maintaining Proper Tension

Every stitch on your needle should be of the same tension. If your second-color stitches are too tight, your garment will pucker. If they are too loose, your pattern stitches will be too large. To avoid this problem, test the tension by spreading your stitches out along your needle every so often to see that all the stitches are of the same tightness.

Stretching the stitches to check the tension.

If this is your first project using this technique, I suggest you cast on a few stitches of some waste yarn and practice until you think you are knitting with both yarns in a nice even tension. Be sure to test your tension as you do when working with two colors.

In this book you will normally use only two colors in any given row. Do not break your secondary yarn color unless you will not be using that color again for many rows. (Example: You will usually break the yarn after the border but you will not break the yarn between rows of dots.) The spacings between the color rows are designed in a way that requires you to break your yarn in only a few places.

□ Floats

Floats are the strands of yarn that run along the wrong (purl) side of your work while you are knitting yarn of another color. Floats longer than 4 stitches are likely to get caught in your fingers when you put on your garment. They also tend to distort the tension of your final garment. Since some of the picture patterns in this book have floats longer than 20 stitches, you'll need to twist the yarn of the color you are not working around the color yarn you are knitting every 3rd of 4th stitch. See illustration below:

Twist

Twisting yarn to catch long floats.

The photo below shows what the wrong side of your work will look like as you go along. I know you will enjoy watching the designs emerge from your knitting needles.

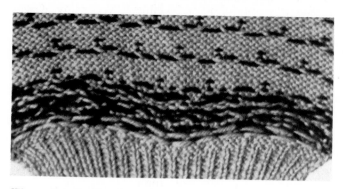

Wrong (purl) side of sweater piece.

□ Embroidering a Third Color

If you need only a small area of one color in your sweater piece, you may wish to embroider the color onto the sweater. This will save you from carrying an extra yarn as you knit.

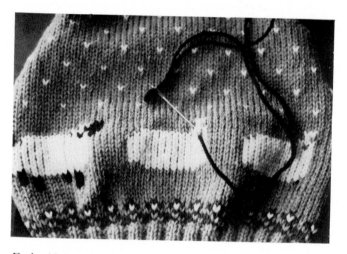

Embroidering a second color.

□ Materials, Tools & Tips

For any garment, good materials result in a better finished product. Because the quality, weight and texture of the yarns you use affect the size and drape of your garment, you must also use materials that are appropriate for your pattern. Knitting projects, while very enjoyable in themselves, cost time and money. Your best results will be achieved by using the yarns suggested by your pattern designer.

□ Recommended Yarns

All of the sweaters pictured in this book were made with either Germantown 4-ply knitting worsted wool yarn by Brunswick or Mayflower Cotton Helarsgarn. Most of the sweaters shown are made with the wool yarn, although you may use the cotton if you prefer. They both knit up in the same gauge and are interchangeable in these designs. If you must use another brand of yarn, please go to a good knitting shop in your area and have the salesperson help you select the proper substitute.

Wool

I will talk about wool first because it is my favorite fiber for sewing and knitting. Wool is prized by knitters for its warmth, elasticity, durability, and ability to hold color. Wool is also one of our most flame-resistant fabrics and is very resistant to dirt and stains.

I have chosen the Germantown wool for several reasons. I love knitting up lots of different color combinations and Germantown is available in a wide range of colors. It is also reasonably priced and readily available in most areas. This yarn is very consistent in thickness from color to color and skein to skein, so I don't have to test my gauge very often when I start a new project with this yarn. The Germantown also works equally well in hand and machine knitting.

I prefer to hand wash all my wool sweaters in cool water. I use regular human shampoo, squeezing the suds through the sweater. I also shampoo and rinse twice. Then I roll the sweater in a towel to remove the excess moisture. I dry my sweaters on a towel on the top of a wire dog crate, but a drying rack works jut as well. This allows the moisture to evaporate from both above and below the sweater. Always read the care instructions that come with your yarn.

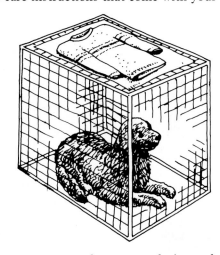

Dry your sweaters on a dog crate or drying rack.

Care of Wool Sweaters

The Germantown yarn is moth-proof, but I have found, to my dismay, that it is not mouse-proof. I live in the country and we get mice in the fall, so I keep my sweaters folded in sweater boxes. Sweaters don't like to hung up on hangers.

Cotton

The wide variety of cotton yarns on the market today hold their shape much better than they used to. Elastic thread, available from your yarn shop, can be knit together with your yarn to help your ribbings keep their shape.

Cotton fabric breathes, making it comfortable in hot weather. It also takes dyes very well and is more flame resistant than most synthetic fibers, making it more suitable for children's garments.

I chose the Mayflower Cotton Helarsgarn because it comes in lovely colors and can be knit in the correct gauge for these sweaters. This yarn is also machine washable.

Tools

All the sweaters in this book can be knit with the same sets of needles: one pair size 5, one pair size 2, and one set (4) size 2 double-pointed needles. I like to use the shortest needles possible for each project, so I often use a round needle, even for straight knitting. They seem to alleviate arm fatigue.

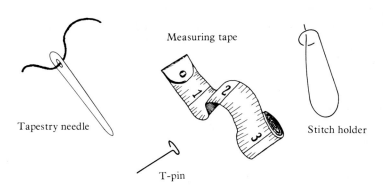

Some helpful tools.

You will also need three stitch holders and a tapestry needle for finishing your garments and embroidering yarn onto your sweater. I keep a measuring tape handy for checking my garment length as I work. I use large T-pins for blocking and for pinning my garment together. They are less likely to get lost than smaller straight pins.

Gauge

Your knitting gauge is the one factor which will determine the final size of your sweater. I can't stress too strongly how important gauge is. When I first started knitting, I thought gauge was some quality of the yarn itself. If the yarn wrapper said 4 stitches to the inch on a size 10 needle, I not only thought I could only get 4 stitches to the inch, I also thought I could only use a size 10 needle. I never took Home Economics in school!

Gauge is a Personal Thing

Gauge is actually the tension at which you knit your stitches. The needles and yarn recommended in a knitting pattern will place most knitters within range of the gauge needed to knit the pattern, but you can use any size needles as long as your gauge is accurate.

My sister Bridget, a doctor by profession, had a terrible time with gauge when she made her first patterned sweater. The pattern directions she had were two sizes too big, so she decided to compensate for the size difference by using a smaller needle than the directions called for. Dr. Bridget, who knits very tightly, never tested her gauge.

When the sweater was finished, she somehow managed to get it on, but no matter how she struggled, she just couldn't get it off. Just picture three Cosgrove sisters — laughing and crying at the same time — as we performed the surgical procedure of cutting her sweater off with scissors. The sweater was a waste of my sister's time and money, but it's made a great family story. Be sure to check your gauge!

Testing Your Gauge

You must make a test of your gauge, measuring at least 1 inch below your knitting needle, to see how close you are to the required gauge for your project. If your tension is too tight, you must either use a larger needle or practice knitting more loosely. If your tension is too loose, you must either use a smaller needle or practice knitting more tightly.

Mistakes in gauge are costly and frustrating.

□ *Tips For Ensuring Proper Fit*

This section will help you make sure that your sweaters fit properly. The sizing in the directions is based on average figure shapes, plus certain allowances for ease of wear. The sweaters in this book are generously proportioned, and because a sweater is not a closely tailored garment, most people will be able to make and wear the sweaters just as they are sized in the instructions.

Since most sweaters are sized by chest measurement, most pattern adjustments are made in the length rather than the width of the sweater. (Both petite and tall women may have a size 32 chest measurement, but they probably won't fit in the same size 32 garment.)

Many children's sweaters will also need alterations. A tall, thin eight-year-old, for instance, may need a size 10 sweater with extra length in the arms and body.

Problems with width do occasionally occur. A large-chested person with a very small waist or a pear-shaped person with narrow shoulders may both want width adjustments in certain areas of their sweaters. A garment that fits properly is flattering to any figure.

Following is a table you may want to use when fitting very large people or people with physical disabilities.

Measurement Table for Special Figure Requirements

Measurement	+	Amount added for Ease*	=	Final Measurement
Back length (collar to waist)		7 in. for adults 5 in. for children size 6 & up		_____
		3 in. for children size 4 & under		_____
Arm length (edge of shoulder to wrist bone)		2 in. + rib length for adults		_____
		1 in. + rib length for children		_____
Chest		3 in. adults 2 in. children		_____
Waist		Same as for Chest		_____
Biceps**		4 in. adults 3 in. children		_____

*These ease measurements are given to help you fit the sweaters in this book. Garments not in this book may require different additions for ease.

**You will not usually be required to make a bicep measurement unless you are knitting for a very large person.

□ *Lengthening or Shortening Your Garment*

You increase or decrease the length of your garment by simply adding or subtracting more rows. This is always done in the area between the top and bottom borders. If this area contains a picture pattern, make the proper adjustment after you have completed the picture pattern. If this area contains rows of dots, you can add or subtract anywhere, but always be sure you have four plain rows between the borders and the dots and between the rows of dots themselves.

□ *Increasing or Decreasing the Width of Your Garment*

You increase or decrease the width of your garment by adding or subtracting stitches on your needle when you cast on. Therefore, you must know your gauge!

Use this formula to find how many stitches to knit when adjusting patterns to fit:

Stitches per inch × the inches needed = how many stitches to knit.

EXAMPLE:
5½ st per inches × 22 inches needed = 121 stitches needed to knit.

8

Be sure to make your increase or decrease all the way up your piece. Do not add or subtract all the stitches from just one side of your pattern graph. In order to keep the graph balanced, you must add or subtract half the stitches from one side and half from the other.

☐ *Adjusting the Pattern Graphs*

Since most of the designs in this book are suitable for men and women, you may want to adjust a men's pattern graph to a women's, or vice versa. Lengthen or shorten as suggested in the previous section.

Use the width formula to find out how many stitches you will need to have.

Note: For women's sweaters, sizing is based on chest measurements so (if you are adapting a men's pattern graph) you will add or decrease stitches from the chest area downwards, marking the pattern decreases as required for women's sizes in the directions. If you are adapting a women's pattern graph for a man, make your adjustments straight up from the bottom border.

Here is an example of how to adjust a men's size 38-40 to a women's size 30-32. I know from my directions that I need to cast on 90 stitches to make a women's size 30-32, and that I will increase my stitches as I knit until there are 99 stitches on my needle. I know from the men's pattern graph that there are 116 stitches in the cast-on for a men's 38-40 sweater. 116 - 90 = 26 stitches that I need to deduct from the beginning of the sweater. I divide this number by two to find the number of stitches to deduct from each side of the bottom of the graph. 26 ÷ 2 = 13 stitches to deduct from each side of the graph.

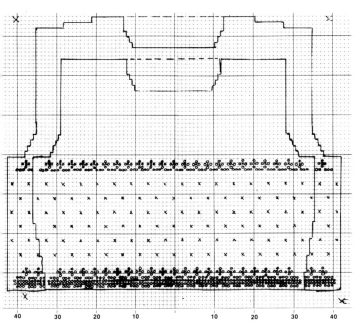

Adjusting a men's size pattern graph to a women's size.

Remembering that I need to increase to 99 stitches in the body of my women's sweater, I add 4 stitches to each side of my graph in the appropriate places as indicated in my women's pattern directions. I must also make the underarm decreases as indicated in my women's directions, so I mark my pattern adjustments all the way up on both sides of the graph.

Be sure to make the proper changes for the sleeve pieces.

☐ *Blocking Pieces*

If your finished pieces look a little bumpy, blocking can help smooth them out. First, tie off any loose yarn (these occur most often where you have switched colors) and weave the ends into the back of the sweater. Place a clean white cotton dishtowel (huck towel) on an ironing borad or a cork board. Place the sweater piece face down on the towel, and pin it flat with T-pins, stretching the sweater piece slightly so it is nice and smooth. Place a *damp* (not wet) pressing cloth on top of the piece, and then press, with your stream iron on a wool setting. Do not move the iron back and forth, simply press down, hold a few seconds, then lift the iron to another spot and press again. Do not press directly on your sweater piece or you may scorch the garment and ruin all your hard work. Let each piece rest until it is cool and dry, then remove the pins and do the next piece.

Pinned and ready to block.

Blocking sweater pieces.

2.

Instructions

Men's Picture Pattern Sweater

Sizes 38 - 40 (42 - 44) (46)

□ Materials

1 pair size 2 needles
1 pair size 5 needles
1 set (4) size 2 double-pointed needles
3 stitch holders
1 tapestry needle

□ Yarn

All of the wool sweaters in this book were made with Germantown 4-ply knitting worsted by Brunswick. The cotton sweaters were made with Mayflower Cotton Helarsgarn.
Amount of Germantown wool yarn needed*:
Background color — 7 skeins (24.5 oz; 685 gms).
Picture pattern color — 1 skein (3.5 oz; 100 gms).
Third, fourth, and fifth colors, if called for — 1 small ball (1 oz; 28 gms).
Amount of Helarsgarn cotton yarn needed*:
Background color — 20 skeins (1000 gms; 35 oz).
Picture pattern color — 4 skeins (200 gms; 7 oz).
Third, fourth, and fifth colors, if called for — 2 skeins (100 gms; 3.5 oz).

* Since the weight of a skein varies from brand to brand, be sure to check the weight if you substitute yarns.

Note: For the following sweaters only you will need an extra skein of the picture pattern color. Piney Woods (p. 98), Maple Leaves (p. 43), and Reindeer (p. 84).

□ Gauge

5½ stitches per inch. **Note:** Test your gauge at least 1 inch below the needle.

□ Stitches

Key to stitches: k = knit; p = purl.

Ribbing Stitch: For front and back pieces, k2, p2; for sleeves and neck, k1, p1.

Stockinette Stitch: Alternate rows of knit (right side) and purl (wrong side).

□ Back

Using size 2 needles, cast on 116 (124) (132) stitches and work in a ribbing of k2, p2 until the work measures 3½ inches from the beginning of the rib.
Now, switch to size 5 needles and knit 1 plain row, increasing 1 stitch in this first row so there are now 117 (125) (133) stitches on the needle. In the next row, begin following the pattern graph, using the bottom border colors where indicated, working in stockinette stitch.
Read the diagram from right to left for knit and from left to right for purl.
Begin the dot pattern (for designs with the picture pattern on the top of the sweater) or the picture pattern (for designs with the picture pattern on the bottom of the sweater) in the 5th row above the last bottom border row.
If you are working the dot pattern here, work a row of dots in every 5th row (as indicated in your pattern graph) until you reach the top border pattern. Make sure there are 4 plain rows between your last row of dots and the first row of your border pattern. **Note:** It is not necessary for you to break the yarn between rows of dots. Let this second color yarn hang loose between rows of dots. Each time you need a row of dots, the yarn will be there for you to pick up again.
When the work measures 17 inches from the beginning, including the rib, begin the top border pattern. Work the top border pattern. Then work 2 plain rows. Then bind off 6 stitches at the beginning of each of the next 2 rows to start the underarm decrease.

In the 5th row above the top border pattern, begin the picture pattern (for designs with the picture pattern on top of the sweater) or the dot pattern (for designs with the picture pattern on the bottom of the sweater) and also continue the underarm decrease by binding off 1 stitch at the beginning of each of the next 8 rows. 97 (105) (113) stitches now remain.

When the work measures 10 inches from the underarm, measuring straight up from the **center** of the work, the back is complete.

Shape the shoulders in the following manner: Bind off 10 (11) (11) (13) stitches at the beginning of each of the next 4 rows. Then bind off 11 (13) (13) stitches at the beginning of each of the next 2 rows. Save the remaining 35 stitches on a stitch holder for the back neck opening.

□ *Front*

Follow the directions as for the back. Do NOT reverse the pattern. When the work measures **8** inches up from the underarm, again measuring straight up from the center of the work, begin to decrease for the Neck opening as follows: Work the first 34 (38) (42) stitches. Then slip the next 29 stitches on a stitch holder (for the front neck opening) and slip the last 34 (38) (42) stitches on a second stitch holder.

Work each side of the neck opening separately. Bind off 1 stitch at the neck edge (every other row) three times. 31 (35) (39) stitches will remain. Continue working the first side until it measures 10 inches up from the underarm (to match the back length). Shape the shoulders in the following manner: Working from the outside edge, bind off 10 (11) (13) stitches every other row 2 times, then also working from the outside edge, bind off the last 11 (13) (13) stitches. Repeat with the 31 (35) (39) stitches on the opposite side of the neck opening.

□ *Sleeves*

With size 2 needles, cast on 52 stitches and work in a ribbing of k1, p1 until the work measures 3½ inches from the beginning. Switch to size 5 needles and knit one plain row, increasing in this first row to 65 stitches by knitting the front and back of about every 4th or 5th stitch.

Now begin following the pattern graph as you did for the body of the sweater. When the work measures about 5 inches from the beginning of the rib, increase 1 stitch at the beginning and at the end of every 6th row until there are 85 (89) (89) stitches on the needle. When the sleeve measures 21 inches from the beginning of the rib, work the top border pattern. (For some designs with a picture pattern on the bottom of the sweater, the top border pattern may end a few inches below the 21-inch measurement. Just knit dot rows until the 21-inch measurement is reached, and then begin the underarm decrease.)

Complete the top border pattern, then knit 2 plain rows. Then begin the underarm decrease by binding off 6 stitches at the beginning of each of the next 2 rows. Start your top picture pattern (or dots) in the 5th row above the top border pattern. The top of the sleeve is shaped by binding off 1 stitch at the beginning of every row until 33 stitches remain. Next, bind off 3 stitches at the beginning of each of the next rows. Bind off the remaining 21 stitches.

□ *Blocking*

If necessary, block pieces according to directions on page 9.

□ *Assembly*

Sew the front to the back at the shoulder seams using a running backstitch. With size 2 double-pointed needles, pick up and knit 88 stitches around the neck (35 from the back stitch holder, 29 from the front stitch holder, and 12 from each side of the neck opening). Work around in a rib of k1, p1 for 9 rows. Bind off loosely.

Now sew the side seams and the arm seams. Sleeves are most easily set in by matching the underarm seams first (with right sides together) and pinning the sleeves in place with large T-pins. Sew the sleeves in using a running backstitch. Tie off and weave in all loose ends.

Women's Picture Pattern Sweater

Sizes 30 - 32 (34 - 36) (38 - 40)

□ **Materials**

1 pair size 2 needles
1 pair size 5 needles
1 set (4) size 2 double-pointed needles
3 stitch holders
1 tapestry needle

□ **Yarn**

All of the wool sweaters in this book were made with Germantown 4-ply knitting worsted by Brunswick. The cotton sweaters were made with Mayflower Cotton Helarsgarn.

Amount of Germantown wool yarn needed*:
Background color — 6 skeins (21 oz; 600 gms).
Picture pattern color -– 1 skein (2.5 oz; 70 gms).
Third, fourth, and fifth colors, if called for — 1 small ball (1 oz; 28 gms).

Amount of Helarsgarn cotton yarn needed*:
Background color — 16 skeins (800 gms; 28 oz).
Picture pattern color — 4 skeins (200 gms; 7 oz).
Third, fourth, and fifth colors, if called for — 2 skeins (100 gms; 3.5 oz).

* Since the weight of a skein varies from brand to brand, be sure to check the weight if you substitute yarns.

Note: For the Tulip sweater only (p. 77), you will need one full skein of the third color.

□ **Gauge**

5½ stitches per inch. **Note:** Test your gauge at least 1 inch below the needle.

□ **Stitches**

Key to stitches: k = knit; p = purl.

Ribbing Stitch: For front and back pieces, k2, p2; for sleeves and neck, k1, p1.

Stockinette Stitch: Alternate rows of knit (right side) and purl (wrong side).

□ **Back**

Using size 2 needles, cast on 90 (94) (98) stitches and work in a ribbing of k2, p2 until the work measures 3 inches from the beginning of the rib.

Now, switch to size 5 needles and knit 1 plain row, increasing 1 stitch in this first row so there are now 91 (95) (99) stitches on the needle. In the next row, begin following the pattern graph, using the bottom border colors where indicated, working in stockinette stitch.

Read the diagram from right to left for knit and from left to right for purl.

Begin the dot pattern (for designs with the picture pattern on the top of the sweater) or the picture pattern (for designs with the picture pattern on the bottom of the sweater) in the 5th row above the last bottom border row.

If you are working the dot pattern here, work a row of dots in every 5th row (as indicated in your pattern graph) until you reach the top border pattern. Make sure there are 4 plain rows between your last row of dots and the first row of your border pattern. **Note:** It is not necessary for you to break the yarn between rows of dots. Let this second color yarn hang loose between rows of dots. Each time you need a row of dots, the yarn will be there for you to pick up again.

When the work measures about 5 inches from the beginning of the rib, increase 1 stitch at the beginning and the end of the needle, and in every 6th row thereafter, until there are 99 (103) (107) stitches on the needle.

When the work measures 15 inches from the beginning of the rib, begin the top border pattern. After the top border pattern is finished, work 2 plain rows. Then bind off 6 stitches at the beginning of each of the next 2 rows to start the underarm decrease.

In the 5th row above the top border pattern, begin the picture pattern (for designs with the picture pattern on top of the sweater) or the dot pattern (for designs with the picture pattern on the bottom of the sweater) and also continue the underarm decrease by binding off 1 stitch at the beginning of each of the next 8 rows. 79 (83) (87) stitches now remain.

When the work measures 7½ (8, 8½) inches from the underarm, measuring straight up from the **center** of the work, the back is complete.

Now bind off 23 (25) (27) stitches, slip the next 33 stitches on a stitch holder (for the back of the neck) and then bind off the remaining 23 (25) (27) stitches.

□ **Front**

Follow the directions as for the back. Do NOT reverse the pattern. When the work measures **6 (6½, 7)** inches up from the underarm, again measuring straight up from the center of the work, begin to decrease for the Neck opening as follows: Work the first 26 (28) (30) stitches. Then slip the next 27 stitches on a stitch holder (for the front neck opening) and slip the last 26 (28) (30) stitches on a second stitch holder.

Work each side of the neck opening separately. Bind off 1 stitch at the neck edge (every other row) three times. 23 (25) (27) stitches will remain. Continue working the first side until it measures 7½ (8, 8½) inches up from the underarm (to match the back length). Bind off. Repeat with the 26 (28) (30) stitches on the opposite side of the neck opening.

□ Sleeves

With size 2 needles, cast on 48 stitches and work in a ribbing of k1, p1 until the work measures 3 inches from the beginning. Switch to size 5 needles and knit one plain row, increasing this row to 61 stitches by knitting the front and back of about every 3rd or 4th stitch.

Now begin following the pattern graph as you did for the body of the sweater. When the work measures about 5 inches from the beginning of the rib, increase 1 stitch at the beginning and at the end of every 6th row until there are 77 (81) (85) stitches on the needle. When the sleeve measures 20 inches from the beginning of the rib, work the top border pattern. (For some designs with a picture pattern on the bottom of the sweater, the top border pattern may end a few inches below the 20-inch measurement. Just knit plain rows until the 20-inch measurement is reached, and then begin the underarm decrease.)

Complete the top border pattern, then knit 2 plain rows. Then begin the underarm decrease by binding off 6 stitches at the beginning of each of the next 2 rows. Start your top picture pattern (or dots) in the 5th row above the top border pattern. The top of the sleeve is shaped by binding off 1 stitch at the beginning of every row until 33 stitches remain. Next, bind off 3 stitches at the beginning of each of the next 4 rows. Bind off the remaining 21 stitches.

□ Blocking

If necessary, block pieces according to directions on page 9.

□ Assembly

Sew the front to the back at the shoulder seams using a running backstitch. With size 2 double-pointed needles, pick up and knit 80 stitches around the neck (33 from the back stitch holder, 27 from the front stitch holder, and 10 from each side of the neck opening). Work around in a rib of k1, p1 for 9 rows. Bind off loosely.

Now sew the side seams and the arm seams. Sleeves are most easily set in by matching the underarm seams first (with right sides together) and pinning the sleeves in place with large T-pins. Sew the sleeves in using a running backstitch. Tie off and weave in all loose ends.

Children's Picture Pattern Sweater

Sizes 8 (10) (12)

□ Materials

1 pair size 2 needles
1 pair size 5 needles
1 set (4) size 2 double-pointed needles
3 stitch holders
1 tapestry needle

□ Yarn

All of the wool sweaters in this book were made with Germantown 4-ply knitting worsted by Brunswick. The cotton sweaters were made with Mayflower Cotton Helarsgarn.

Amount of Germantown wool yarn needed★:
Background color — 4 skeins (14 oz; 400 gms).
Picture pattern color — 1 skein (3.5 oz; 100 gms).
Third, fourth, and fifth colors, if called for — 1 small ball (1 oz; 28 gms).

Amount of Helarsgarn cotton yarn needed★:
Background color — 10 skeins (500 gms; 17.5 oz).

Picture pattern color — 2 skeins (100 gms; 3.5 oz).
Third, fourth, and fifth colors, if called for — 2 skeins (100 gms; 3.5 oz).

★ Since the weight of a skein varies from brand to brand, be sure to check the weight if you substitute yarns.

□ Gauge

5½ stitches per inch. **Note:** Test your gauge at least 1 inch below the needle.

□ Stitches

Key to stitches: k = knit; p = purl.

Ribbing Stitch: For front and back pieces, k2, p2; for sleeves and neck, k1, p1.

Stockinette Stitch: Alternate rows of knit (right side) and purl (wrong side).

13

□ Back

Using size 2 needles, cast on 80 (84) (88) stitches and work in a ribbing of k2, p2 until the work measures 2½ inches from the beginning of the rib. Now, switch to size 5 needles and knit 1 plain row, increasing 1 stitch in this first row so there are now 81 (85) (89) stitches on the needle. In the next row, begin following the pattern graph, using the bottom border colors where indicated, working in stockinette stitch.

Read the diagram from right to left for knit and from left to right for purl.

Begin the dot pattern (for designs with the picture pattern on the top of the sweater) or the picture pattern (for designs with the picture pattern on the bottom of the sweater) in the 5th row above the last bottom border row.

If you are working the dot pattern here, work a row of dots in every 5th row, as indicated in your pattern graph, until you reach the top border pattern. Make sure there are 4 plain rows between your last row of dots and the first row of your border pattern. **Note:** It is not necessary for you to break the yarn between rows of dots. Let this second color yarn hang loose between rows of dots. Each time you need a row of dots, the yarn will be there for you to pick up again.

When the work measures about 11 (12) (13) inches from the beginning (including the rib), begin your top border pattern. Work the top border pattern, then work 2 plain rows. Next, bind off 4 stitches at the beginning of each of the next 2 rows to start the underarm decrease.

In the 5th row above the top border pattern, begin the picture pattern (for designs with the picture pattern on top of the sweater) or the dot pattern (for designs with the picture pattern on the bottom of the sweater) and also continue the underarm decrease by binding off 1 stitch at the beginning of each of the next 4 rows. 69 (73) (77) stitches now remain.

When the work measures 6 (6½) (7) inches up from the underarm, measuring straight up from the **center** of the work, the back is complete. Bind off 19 (21) (23) stitches at the beginning of each of the next 2 rows. Place the remaining 31 stitches on a stitch holder for the back neck opening.

□ Front

Follow the directions as for the back. Do NOT reverse the pattern. When the work measures 4½ (5) (5½) inches up from the underarm, again measuring straight up from the center of the work, begin to decrease for the front neck opening as follows: Work the first 22 (24) (26) stitches. Then slip the next 25 stitches on a stitch holder (for the front neck opening) and slip the last 22 (24) (26) stitches on a second stitch holder.

Work each side of the neck opening separately. Bind off 1 stitch at the neck edge (every other row) three times. 19 (21) (23) stitches will remain. Continue working the first side until it measures 6 (6½) (7) inches up from the underarm (to match the back length). Bind off. Repeat with the 22 (24) (26) stitches on the opposite side of the neck opening.

□ Sleeves

With size 2 needles, cast on 44 stitches and work in a ribbing of k1, p1 until the work measures 2½ inches from the beginning. Switch to size 5 needles and knit one plain row, increasing this row to 53 stitches by knitting the front and back of about every 3rd or 4th stitch.

Now begin following the pattern graph as you did for the body of the sweater. When the work measures about 4 inches from the beginning of the rib, increase 1 stitch at the beginning and at the end of every 6th row until there are 65 (69) (73) stitches on the needle. When the sleeve measures 14 (15) (16) inches from the beginning of the rib, work the top border pattern. Complete the top border pattern, then knit 2 plain rows. Then begin the underarm decrease by binding off 4 stitches at the beginning of each of the next 2 rows. Start your top picture pattern (or dots) in the 5th row above the top border pattern. The top of the sleeve is shaped by binding off 1 stitch at the beginning of every row until 27 stitches remain. Next, bind off 3 stitches at the beginning of each of the next 4 rows. Bind off the remaining 15 stitches.

□ Blocking

If necessary, block pieces according to directions on page 9.

□ Assembly

Sew the front to the back at the shoulder seams using a running backstitch. With size 2 double-pointed needles, pick up and knit 76 stitches around the neck (31 from the back stitch holder, 25 from the front stitch holder and 10 from each side of the neck opening). Work around in a rib of k1, p1 for 7 rows. Bind off loosely.

Now sew the side seams and the arm seams. Sleeves are most easily set in by matching the underarm seams first (with right sides together) and pinning the sleeves in place with large T-pins. Sew the sleeves in using a running backstitch. Tie off and weave in all loose ends.

Children's Picture Pattern Sweater

Sizes 2 (4) (6)

□ Materials

1 pair size 2 needles
1 pair size 5 needles
1 set (4) size 2 double-pointed needles
3 stitch holders
1 tapestry needle

□ Yarn

All of the wool sweaters in this book were made with Germantown 4-ply knitting worsted by Brunswick. The cotton sweaters were made with Mayflower Cotton Helarsgarn.

Amount of Germantown wool yarn needed★:
Background color — 3 skeins (10.5 oz; 300 gms).
Picture pattern color — 1 skein (3.5 oz; 100 gms).
Third, fourth, and fifth colors, if called for — 1 small ball (1 oz; 28 gms).

Amount of Helarsgarn cotton yarn needed★:
Background color — 8 skeins (400 gms; 14 oz).
Picture pattern color — 2 skeins (100 gms; 3.5 oz).
Third, fourth, and fifth colors, if called for — 2 skeins (100 gms; 3.5 oz).

★ Since the weight of a skein varies from brand to brand, be sure to check the weight if you substitute yarns.

□ Gauge

5½ stitches per inch. **Note:** Test your gauge at least 1 inch below the needle.

□ Stitches

Key to stitches: k = knit; p = purl.

Ribbing Stitch: For front and back pieces, k2, p2; for sleeves and neck, k1, p1.

Stockinette Stitch: Alternate rows of knit (right side) and purl (wrong side).

□ Back

Using size 2 needles, cast on 62 (66) (70) stitches and work in a ribbing of k2, p2 until the work measures 2 inches from the beginning of the rib. Now, switch to size 5 needles and knit 1 plain row, increasing 1 stitch in this first row so there are now 63 (67) (71) stitches on the needle. In the next row, begin following the pattern graph, using the bottom border colors where indicated, working in stockinette stitch.

Read the diagram from right to left for knit and from left to right for purl.

Begin the dot pattern (for designs with the picture pattern on the top of the sweater) or the picture pattern (for designs with the picture pattern on the bottom of the sweater) in the 5th row above the last bottom border row.

If you are working the dot pattern here, work a row of dots in every 5th row, as indicated in your pattern graph, until you reach the top border pattern. Make sure there are 4 plain rows between your last row of dots and the first row of your border pattern. **Note:** It is not necessary for you to break the yarn between rows of dots. Let this second color yarn hang loose between rows of dots. Each time you need a row of dots, the yarn will be there for you to pick up again.

When the work measures about 8 (9) (10) inches from the beginning (including the rib), begin your top border pattern. Work the top border pattern, then work 2 plain rows. Next, bind off 3 stitches at the beginning of each of the next 2 rows to start the underarm decrease.

In the 5th row above the top border pattern, begin the picture pattern (for designs with the picture pattern on top of the sweater) or the dot pattern (for designs with the picture pattern on the bottom of the sweater) and also continue the underarm decrease by binding off 1 stitch at the beginning of each of the next 4 rows. 53 (57) (61) stitches now remain.

When the work measures 5 (5½) (6) inches up from the underarm, measuring straight up from the **center** of the

work, the back is complete. Bind off 13 (15) (17) stitches at the beginning of each of the next 2 rows. Place the remaining 27 stitches on a stitch holder for the back neck opening.

□ Front

Follow the directions as for the back. Do NOT reverse the pattern. When the work measures 3½ (4) (4½) inches up from the underarm, again measuring straight up from the center of the work, begin to decrease for the front neck opening as follows: Work the first 16 (18) (20) stitches. Then slip the next 21 stitches on a stitch holder (for the front neck opening) and slip the last 16 (18) (20) stitches on a second stitch holder.

Work each side of the neck opening separately. Bind off 1 stitch at the neck edge (every other row) three times. 13 (15) (17) stitches should remain. Continue working the first side until it measures 5 (5½) (6) inches up from the underarm (to match the back length). Bind off. Repeat with the 16 (18) (20) stitches on the opposite side of the neck opening.

□ Sleeves

With size 2 needles, cast on 40 stitches and work in a ribbing of k1, p1 until the work measures 2 inches from the beginning. Switch to size 5 needles and knit one plain row, increasing this row to 45 stitches by knitting the front and back of about every 6th stitch.

Now begin following the pattern graph as you did for the body of the sweater. When the work measures about 3 inches from the beginning of the rib, increase 1 stitch at the beginning and at the end of every 7th row until there are 53 (57) (61) stitches on the needle. When the sleeve measures 11 (12) (13) inches from the beginning of the rib, work the top border pattern. Complete the top border pattern, then knit 2 plain rows. Then begin the underarm decrease by binding off 3 stitches at the beginning of each of the next 2 rows. Start your top picture pattern (or dots) in the 5th row above the top border pattern. The top of the sleeve is shaped by binding off 1 stitch at the beginning of every row until 27 stitches remain. Next, bind off 3 stitches at the beginning of each of the next 4 rows. Bind off the remaining 15 stitches.

□ Blocking

If necessary, block pieces according to directions on page 9.

□ Assembly

Sew the front to the back at the shoulder seams using a running backstitch. With size 2 double-pointed needles, pick up and knit 68 stitches around the neck (27 from the back stitch holder, 21 from the front stitch holder and 10 from each side of the neck opening). Work around in a rib of k1, p1 for 5 rows. Bind off loosely.

Now sew the side seams and the arm seams. Sleeves are most easily set in by matching the underarm seams first (with right sides together) and pinning the sleeves in place with large T-pins. Sew the sleeves in using a running backstitch. Tie off and weave in all loose ends.

3.

Machine Knitting

These instructions and hints are provided to help machine knitters make the sweaters in this book and it is assumed they already know how to use their knitting machine. Any good bulky knitting machine should work, such as the Knitking PC Bulky or the Brother KH 260E. (I use the Knitking PC Bulky.) Please refer to your machine's instruction booklet or your salesperson if you have another brand of bulky machine to be sure these projects are adaptable to your machine.

If you are just now shopping for a knitting machine, you may find that some salespeople say you can knit bulkier yarns, such as the 4-ply knitting worsted used in these designs, on a fine-gauge machine by using every other needle in the needle bed. I have spent many hours trying to get this technique to work, with totally unsatisfactory results. If this claim is made to you, please ask for a demonstration. Purchase the type of machine that will best suit your needs and tastes.

For some of the designs in the book, such as the Reindeer, you will be able to use 24-stitch pattern repeat punch cards for the entire design. Others, such as the children's Newfie & Pups sweater, will require a combination of punch card and hand-pulled needles.

□ *Machine Knitting Chart*

Gauge _____ at tension dial setting _____
Cast on _____ st. for size _____
_____ rows/inch
_____ rows from A to B (beginning of bottom border to beginning of top border)
_____ rows from B to C (for top border)
_____ rows from C to D (from end of top border to bind-off)
_____ rows from A to B (for arm)

□ *About Machine Knitting Directions*

There are no specific machine knitting directions for the sweaters in this book. Instead, machine knitters will have to adapt the picture pattern graphs and the hand knitting directions for machine use. Pages 124 - 127 have blank graphs to record your conversions.

At the end of this section there is an in-depth example of how to adapt hand-knitting directions for machine use.

Machine knitters usually end up working from hand-knitting directions for two reasons. First, machine knitting directions are often difficult to read, increasing the chances for mistakes. (Since there's almost no way to see a mistake in dimensions when your piece is stretched out on your knitting machine, avoiding mistakes is very important.) The second, and most important reason, is that yarns and machines vary so much that it is virtually impossible for machine knitting directions to give an accurate tension dial setting or number of rows to count.

Although gauge can usually be figured accurately by making test swatches, the rows per inch (vertical measurement) on your swatch may not match your required gauge. This means that the machine knitter has to go through the machine knitting directions and convert every vertical measurement to the correct number of rows.

□ *Conversion Formulas*

This section has two simple formulas for converting inches to stitches and inches to rows:

Stitches per inch x inches needed = stitches needed.
Rows per inch x inches needed = rows needed.

Here is a formula for converting gauge to gauge to get stitches to knit.
1.   Divide the number of stitches in the pattern directions by the gauge in the pattern directions to find the inches (the

width you want).

2. Multiply the number of inches by the desired gauge to get the number of stitches you will need.

You will use the gauge-to-gauge formula when a pattern's directions call for a greater number of stitches to knit than are available on your needle bed. Since you will usually be decreasing your gauge, try the next smallest gauge first.

Example:
1. 107 stitches ÷ 5.5 stitches per inch = 19.5 inches
2. 19.5 inches x 5.0 stitches per inch = 97 stitches to knit.

❏ Gauge

The hand-knitting instructions and the picture pattern graphs in this book are all designed to be knit at a gauge of 5½ stitches per inch. You will machine knit all the sweaters at this gauge EXCEPT for the men's sizes. This is because the needle bed will not accommodate the number of stitches needed at 5½ stitches per inch for these sizes.

❏ Making Your Swatches

Knit several swatches, each at a different tension dial setting. Label the dial settings on the swatches, and let them rest overnight. You may be excited and not want to wait, but your swatches won't be any good unless they have had a chance to relax into their normal sizes. Pick out the swatch with the correct gauge and record the rows per inch. We will use this figure later.

Once you find the proper tension dial number for your desired gauge, you know how wide your garment will be when you knit a certain number of stitches across your machine.

For the men's size sweaters in this book, use the following table to find the correct gauge and number of stitches when converting the hand-knitting directions.

Men's Machine Gauge Table

Men's size	Gauge	Front & Back	Sleeve at widest point ★
38 - 40	5 st. per inch	105 st.	77 st.
42 - 44	5 st. per inch	115 st.	81 st.
46	4½ st. per inch	111 st.	79 st.

Always make your men's sleeve ribs at 52 stitches and increase in the first row after the rib to 65 stitches. They work out just fine.

❏ Gauge Mistakes = Gauge Disasters

The table above should demonstrate to you how important gauge really is. If you think about it, you will realize that if your gauge is off just 1 stitch per inch, you could end up with a much smaller or larger sweater.

❏ Adapting Pattern Graphs For Machine Knitting

Choose a design in this book and mark the changes for machine knitting on your correct set of hand-knitting directions. Then, turn to the picture pattern graph for the sweater that you wish to knit. Write the number of stitches

you need, the size, tension dial setting, and rows-per-inch figures for your project on the Machine Knitting Chart.

If your number of stitches to knit is different from those on the pattern graph, mark off the correct number of stitches to knit on the picture pattern graph. Be sure to add or subtract the same number of stitches on each side of the graph.

❏ Ribbings

You will notice that all the picture graphs and the Men's Machine Gauge Table start in the first row of knitting after the ribbings. Because I want my machine knit sweaters to look as hand-knit as possible, I always knit my ribs by hand after each piece is finished.

If you prefer to make machine ribbing, I suggest you make the piece without the rib first, then take it off the machine, remove your waste yarn, then re-hang your piece, upside-down, on the needle bed, and then make your ribbing. If you do your ribbing first, the stretching from your cast-on comb, and the pulling from your weights, may destroy the rib yarn's elasticity.

❏ Catching Floats With A Transfer Tool

Floats are the strands of yarn that run along the inside of your piece while yarn of another color is being knit. Floats of a length of more than 4 stitches tend to distort the tension of your finished garment and are likely to get caught in your fingers when putting on your sweater. Since some of the picture patterns have floats of 20 stitches or more, use the following directions to prevent problems.

Knit 1 patterned row and then the 2nd patterned row. Now refer back to the first row you have knit and find the floats that are more than 4 stitches wide. Using your single transfer tool, split your float yarn and transfer two strands of your 4-ply yarn to the needle bed at about every third or fourth needle along the length of the float. Continue in this manner for each row of your picture pattern (and dots) that has floats longer than 4 stitches. In row 3 you will transfer up the floats from row 2; in row 4, the floats from row 3; and so forth. Transferred floats will not normally show on the outside of your garment. If you have two different colored floats from the same row in the same area, alternate these colors when transferring up. In this case, you'd be transferring up at about every second or third needle along the needle bed.

Catching the floats.

View of floats after next row has been knit.

☐ *Knitting In Three Colors*

Normally you will only be working with one or two colors at a time. In a few cases, though, such as most of the border patterns and some of the picture patterns, you will work three colors in the same row. If you have a Brother KH 260E or a Knitking PC Bulky machine, pull your third color needles all the way out to the HOLD position, then knit your row, lay your third color yarn over the hold position needles (needle gates must be open to receive the yarn). Then knit the third color yarn by pushing the HOLD position needles back to working position while maintaining the proper tension on your third color yarn.

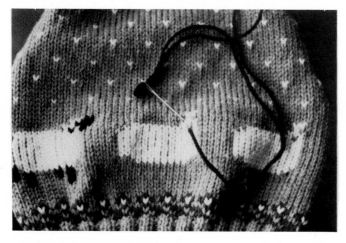

Embroidering a third color.

☐ *Embroidering A Third Color*

In some cases you will need only small areas of a third color, such as in the children's Lamb sweater (see picture illustration). Since I only needed small amounts of black, I knit only the white part of the lamb. Then, when each piece was finished, I embroidered the head, tail, and legs over the background color (white) in black thread. This avoids having to transfer up long floats of the black (third) color.

☐ *Weights*

Adequate weights will help you knit a better garment. In addition to the claw weights provided with my machine, I always use at least one large ribber weight for each piece. For large pieces I use two large ribber weights. These are

available from your knitting machine salesperson.

Yarn can be damaged by hanging on your machine too long with the weights on it. Try to allow yourself enough time to finish an entire piece in one sitting. If this is not possible, take all the weights off the cast-on comb and let the fabric relax. (Do not remove the cast-on comb.)

I had just such an emergency one August night when I was up late knitting. My dog, Scarlet, decided to have her puppies a day or so early. Her water broke at 1:00 a.m., and in all the excitement I forgot to take the weights off the sweater. Scarlet had her first puppy at 4:00 a.m. and the last one just after noon that day. Two days later I was able to get back to my knitting and discovered a damaged sweater piece. In the end everything turned out just fine: I learned a valuable lesson and the puppies all found wonderful homes.

☐ *Increasing Stitches*

I like to use the fully-fashioned method pictured in the illustrations below to increase stitches.

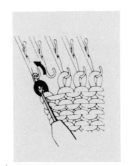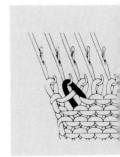

Fully fashioned increase.

☐ *Decreasing Stitches*

I like to use the simple decreasing method pictured in the illustrations below.

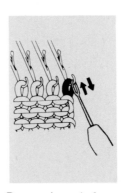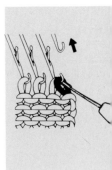

Decreasing stitches.

☐ *Hand-Pulling The Needles*

For all designs in this book with pattern repeats of greater than 24 stitches, you'll have to hand-pull your second color needles out from the working (background color) position to the pattern knitting position in EVERY row of the design.

Always read your pattern graph from right to left. Because you're working on the wrong or purl side of the garment at all times, any designs which you have to hand pull will be reversed when your garment is finished.

Proceed as follows: Read the first pattern graph row and pull pattern needles out to the PATTERN KNITTING position. Knit across. Read the next row and pull the pattern needles out to the PATTERN KNITTING position. Knit across. Now transfer up the floats from the first row to the second row as needed (see section on floats). Pull needles for the third pattern row. Repeat the process until the pattern is finished.

Putting It All Together

You now know how to find your gauge and rows per inch, how to adapt the sweater pattern graphs to machine knitting, knit in three colors, transfer floats, work your punch cards, and hand pull your needles.

This next section will show you how to put all these techniques together.

Combining The Techniques

Let's use for our example the children's Newfie & Pups sweater pictured on page 59. Here's how I would knit the back of the sweater, step-by-step. I chose red for the background color, black for the dogs and dots, and gray and black for my borders. My hand-knitting directions tell me that the length of my piece should be 8 inches from the beginning of the rib to the first row of the top border pattern. I deduct 2 inches for my rib: 8 - 2 = 6. Now I use my formula: 7 rows per inch x 6 inches = 42 rows needed to get from the beginning to my first top border row. There will be 5 inches from my last top border row to the finish of the piece. 7 rows per inch x 5 inches = 35 rows. The border I have chosen has 5 rows, so there will be a total of 42 + 5 + 35 = 82 rows in this piece. Now I mark my pattern graph chart with the appropriate figures.

I always divide the piece up in this fashion: beginning to start of the top border, and end of the top border to the finish of the piece. If I know these rows are right, then I know that all the pieces of my finished garment will fit together properly.

Newfie & Pups (Children's Size 2)

Gauge 5½ stitches per inch and 7 rows per inch at tension dial setting 3. (**Note:** I hand-knit my ribbing when the piece is finished.) Move the carriage to the right side of your machine. Insert the dot punch card and move the punch card lever to the OFF position. Then place the change knob on the carriage in the NORMAL position. Pull out 63 needles (31 left of the 0 position and 32 to the right of the 0 position) to WORKING POSITION. Thread your background yarn into the yarn feeder. Knit one row across. Hang on comb and weights. Knit 4 plain rows (I don't use waste yarn). Set row counter to 0. Now re-set the change knob to KC.

Now thread in your second color (gray), while reading the pattern graph, hand pull the first row of pattern needles out to PATTERN KNITTING position. Knit across. Hand pull the second row of the border pattern and knit across. Repeat for the 3rd row of border pattern. In the 4th row of the border pattern, hand pull the second color (gray) needles to the PATTERN KNITTING position and the third color (black) needles to the HOLD position. Knit across. Now, lay the third color (black) yarn across the open needle gates of the HOLD position needles and push each one back to the WORKING position. Now hand pull and knit the last row of the border pattern.

Knit 3 plain rows. Take second color (gray) yarn out of yarn feeder and replace with third color (black) yarn. Set punch card lever to ON position. Knit 1 row across. "Dot" needles have now moved out to PATTERN KNITTING position. Knit across first pattern row. Knit next row (plain). Transfer the floats up. Repeat until 42 rows have been knit. Be sure there are 4 plain rows between the last row of dots and the first row of the top border pattern. Turn punch card lever to OFF position. Reset dial to beginning mark on the dot card. Remove the third color (black) yarn from the yarn feeder and replace with the second color (gray). Hand pull and knit the top border pattern. Set row counter to 0. Knit 2 plain rows. Bind off 3 stitches at the beginning of each of the next 2 rows. In the 5th row above the last top border row, switch yarn again to your third color (black) and start hand pulling needles for the top picture pattern. Continue decreasing for the underarm by binding off 1 stitch at the beginning of each of the next 4 rows.

When the picture pattern is complete, knit 3 plain rows. Then return punch card lever to ON position and continue knitting until 35 rows have been knit. Bind off 13 stitches at the beginning of each of the next 2 rows. Slip the remaining 27 stitches on a stitch holder for the back neck opening.

Now take the comb and the weights off the piece. Unravel 2 of the bottom 4 rows. Slip the stitches on a size 2 needle and hand-knit a rib of k2, p2 for 2 inches, then bind off all stitches. If you prefer, you may instead transfer the stitches back to your machine and knit your bottom rib with your tension dial at a very low setting (0).

Finishing The Machine Knit Garment

Let all of yor pieces rest overnight to make sure they relax into their final shapes. Then tie off and weave in any loose yarn ends. You will notice that there are some gaps at the outside edges of your picture pattern between the picture pattern yarn and the background color yarn. Thread a tapestry needle with background color yarn and weave the two edges together loosely where needed. Do this on the WRONG side of the work.

Block Pieces

See instructions for blocking.

Assemble Pieces

Assemble pieces as you do for hand-knit garments.

Punch Cards

On the following pages you will find punch cards for many of the designs in this book. These are all 24-stitch pattern repeat cards. You will notice that most of the cards have more than one design on them. Punch cards are expensive, so I like to double up on them whenever possible. I have marked the starting point for each design on the right-hand edge of the card. If you wish to make a punch card for your own design, turn the card over and punch from the back side.

Operate Punch Cards

Insert your punch card and dial the card feeding knob to the starting point indicated on your card. Make sure the card lock lever is in the OFF position. Knit the desired number of plain rows as indicated in your pattern. Now move card lock lever to the ON position and continue knitting.

□ Vertical Pattern Repeats

You will notice that the punch cards for the Maple Leaf and the Tulip patterns have only two vertical repeats of the pattern. In each case, knit one plain row after the second repeat and then dial your card back to your marked starting position. Continue knitting until you have completed the final repeat.

□ Balancing The Design

Remember that your punch cards will keep repeating the design all along your needle bed in both directions from the center. Refer to your pattern graph and push back any unwanted needles from the PATTERN KNITTING position to the WORKING position. These needles will then knit only your background color. Make sure there are always two or three plain (background color) stitches on each side of your work. Your piece will hold its shape better and be easier to assemble. Since you'll always be working with an odd number of stitches on your needle bed, the punch cards are designed so this extra stitch is always on the right-hand side of your needle bed. Use your "dot" punch card for all the sweaters in the book except the baby bags. If you make sure that your extra stitch is on the right-hand side of your needle bed, your dots will always be evenly balanced in every row.

□ Mistakes In Punching Cards

If you make just a few mistakes in punching out your card, you don't have to throw it away. Just put a small piece of tape over your mistake on the back of the card. Then turn the card over and press the little paper circle firmly back into its place.

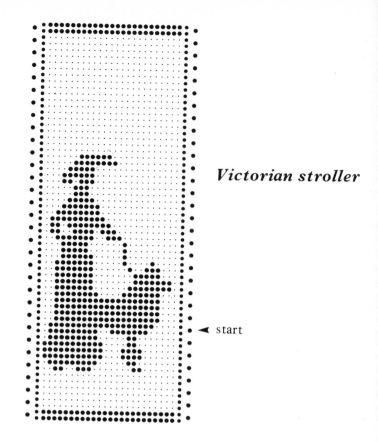

Victorian stroller

◄ start

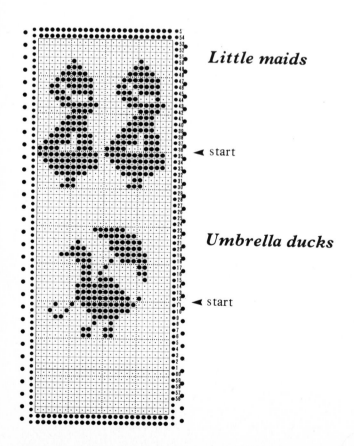

Little maids

◄ start

Umbrella ducks

◄ start

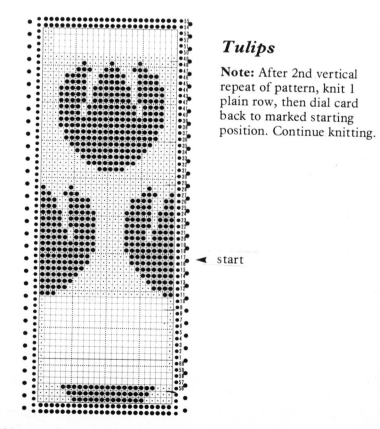

Tulips

Note: After 2nd vertical repeat of pattern, knit 1 plain row, then dial card back to marked starting position. Continue knitting.

◄ start

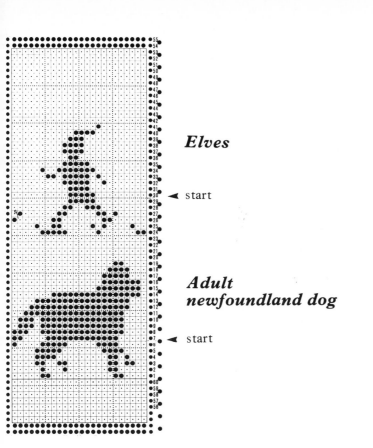

Elves

◄ start

*Adult
newfoundland dog*

◄ start

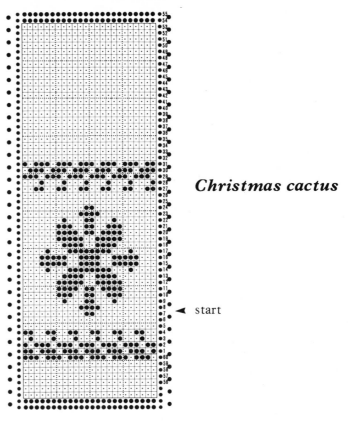

Christmas cactus

◄ start

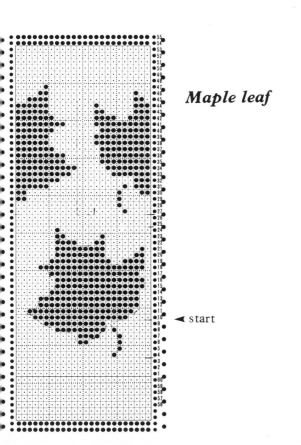

Maple leaf

◄ start

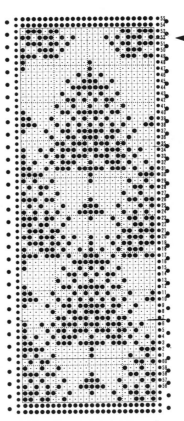

◄ start

Piney woods

Note: There are 5 vertical repeats of the pine trees. In the last repeat you want to knit in only the tops of the trees of the 5th repeat. Therefore, push back the needles from what would be the beginning of the 6th repeat to working (background color) position.

Start on 35 for 5 repeats.

Start on 53 for 4 repeats. (women's sizes)

21

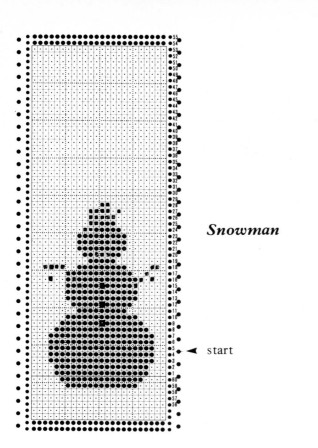

Snowman

◄ start

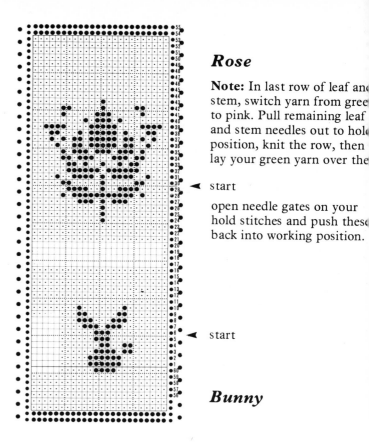

Rose

Note: In last row of leaf and stem, switch yarn from green to pink. Pull remaining leaf and stem needles out to hold position, knit the row, then lay your green yarn over the

◄ start

open needle gates on your hold stitches and push these back into working position.

◄ start

Bunny

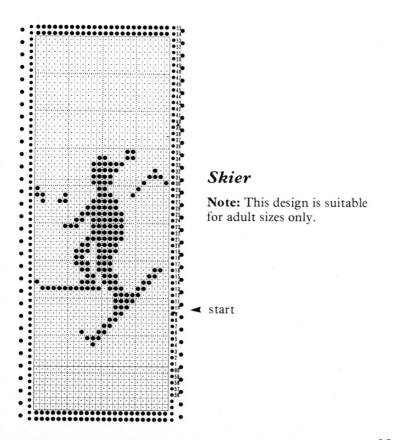

Skier

Note: This design is suitable for adult sizes only.

◄ start

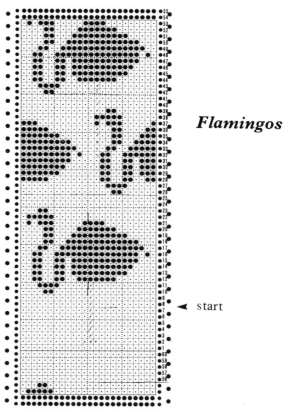

Flamingos

◄ start

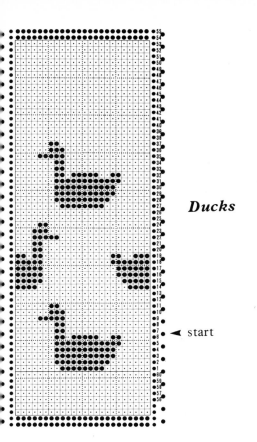

Ducks

◄ start

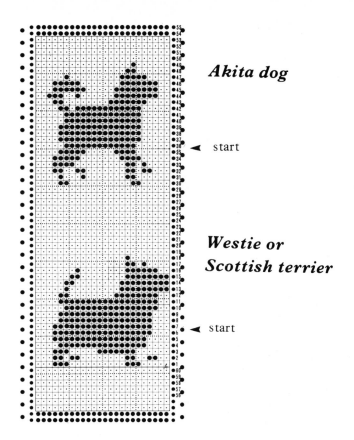

Akita dog

◄ start

Westie or
Scottish terrier

◄ start

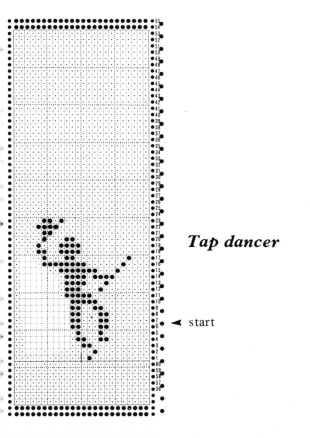

Tap dancer

◄ start

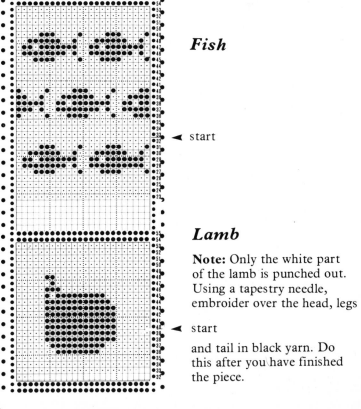

Fish

◄ start

Lamb

Note: Only the white part of the lamb is punched out. Using a tapestry needle, embroider over the head, legs

◄ start

and tail in black yarn. Do this after you have finished the piece.

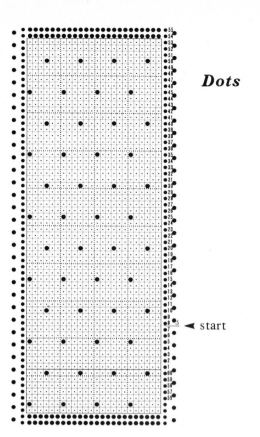

Dots

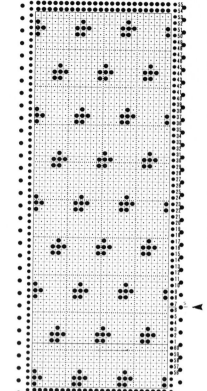

◀ start

All-over rosebuds for Rose design & Little maids baby bag

Note: In every first row of rosebud design there are two stitches. The stitch on the left is for the leaf (3rd color). Pull this needle out to hold position, then knit your row, then lay your green yarn over the open needle gates on your hold stitches and push these needles back to working position.

◀ start

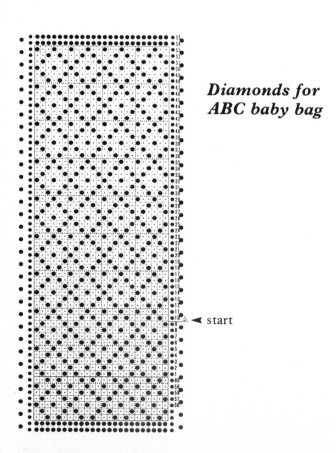

Diamonds for ABC baby bag

◀ start

4.

Creating Your Own Designs

This section of the book will show you how to transform your own designs into a picture pattern sweater. A pencil, several sheets of graph paper, and an intriguing idea are all you need — it's that simple. (Tip: the more graph paper you have on hand, the freer you'll feel to experiment.)

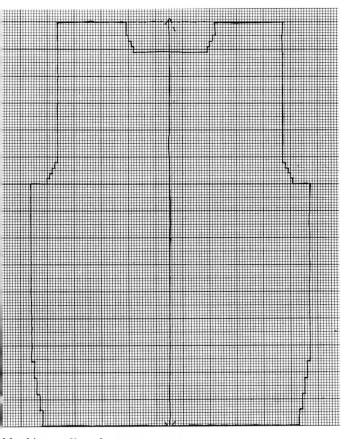

Marking outlines for a sweater piece.

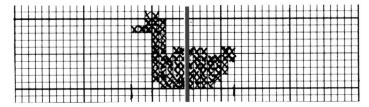

Centering the duck design.

If you're starting from an original sketch, I suggest you knit up a small swatch with the design in it to make sure it looks the way you planned. Knitting stitches are a little longer than they are wide, and it's difficult to visualize exactly how the final product will look from a graph.

When I first graphed out the design for the adult Skiers' pattern shown on page 100, it looked great on paper, but when knitted up it looked like ants on skis. You can often fix your design by simplifying it a little bit. In the case of the Skiers' design, taking out some of the curves in the figure made all the difference.

Another way to personalize your picture knit sweaters is to mix and match design elements from the sweaters in this book. Pages 120 - 123 have additional picture designs, borders, and a knitting alphabet to help you along.

You can also create a design from the photograph of a favorite person, hobby, or pet. Just place a sheet of tissue paper over the photo and trace the basic outline of your subject. Use a second ink color to bring out some detail, and then convert your tracing to a graph. Again, be sure to knit up a swatch of your design and make any necessary adjustments before making your sweater. Children's coloring books are also a good source for simple designs.

Just like an artist with canvas and paints, you will want your design to be nicely balanced. Think of your sweater as the canvas and your yarn as the paint. The design is the entire picture you are creating, which may consist of one large item or several small figures.

I will use a simple duck design to show you — step by step — how to make an interesting sweater. The graph in this example is for a women's size 34-36.

□ *Preparing Your Graph*

Mark off the outlines for a front/back sweater piece on a piece of graph paper, as shown in the illustration. Next, find the center of the bottom row, and mark a line straight up to the top. Use this center line to balance your design.

□ *Borders*

Choose a border design and pencil your borders on the graph. Leave at least 2 or 3 plain stitches on each side of your border for seam allowance. Use your borders as a reference point for placing your picture designs. My own designs usually start in the 3rd or 5th row above the border.

□ *Balancing the Design in the Sweater*

First count the number of stitches across your graph along the bottom and then the number of stitches along the top of the graph above the last underarm decrease. In this example, a woman's size 34-36, there are 95 stitches across the bottom and 75 stitches across the top of the graph. Deduct 4 stitches from each figure for seam allowance. On the bottom: 95 - 4 = 91 stitches available for your design. On the top: 75 - 4 = 74 stitches available for your design.

The duck pattern is 15 stitches wide. 91 — 15 = a maximum of 6 ducks across the bottom of the sweater. Since I will want some space between the ducks, I decide to use only 5 ducks. 5 ducks x 15 stitches per duck = 75 total stitches for ducks. 91 - 75 = 16 stitches left over. I could simply put 4 stitches between each duck (4 x 4 = 16), but I have decided to make 2 plain stitches between each duck and 4 more plain stitches on each side of my pattern graph. Now I re-add to check my math: 6 plain + 15 patterned + 2 plain + 15 patterned + 2 plain + 15 patterned + 2 plain + 15 patterned + 2 plain + 15 patterned + 6 plain stitches = 95 stitches across the bottom of my pattern graph. Repeat this process to find out how many ducks to graph across the top of the sweater.

□ *Marking Your Design on the Graph*

Find your center vertical line and count up 4 rows from the border pattern. Mark in 1 duck in the 5th row above your border pattern. Half of the duck will be on one side of the

vertical line and half will be on the other. Mark in the other 4 ducks, making sure to leave 2 plain rows between ducks.

I have decided to make two more lines of ducks. The second line of ducks will face the opposite direction. Because I know where the center of the duck is, it's easy to turn them around.

To place the second line of ducks, count up 4 plain rows from the first line of ducks and pencil a line across the graph. This line will be the base line for your second line of ducks to sit on. Count off 1 plain stitch to the right of the center vertical line and then pencil in a duck. Mark in the rest of your ducks as before, making sure there are 2 plain stitches between each duck. Six ducks will fit here because the sweater is increasing.

To make a third line of ducks, count up 4 plain rows above the last line and draw another base line for this row of ducks to sit on. The duck in the middle of this line will be in the same position as the middle duck in the first line. Make a pencil line on each side of the middle duck in the first line, straight up and intersecting the base line you have drawn across the graph for the third line of ducks. Pencil in the middle duck first, and then go on to the other 4 ducks, making sure there are 2 plain stitches between each duck. There will be 5 ducks in this line.

Now I have three lines of ducks with plenty of room above them to lengthen or shorten my sweater when I am knitting. I have decided to leave the top of my sweater plain. To make the sleeves match, find the center of the graph and mark off the stitches for the arm — as per your pattern directions — evenly on each side of the vertical line. Leave at least 2 plain stitches on each side of the arm graph for seam allowance.

□ *Color*

The colors you choose can change the whole look of your sweater. For instance, you can easily feminize some of the sweaters in this book designed for men by selecting softer colors.

You may also decide to use two background colors, one for the bottom of the sweater, and one for the top. Tip: Using the darker color on the bottom of the sweater and the lighter color on the top will make your waist appear smaller.

A single row of a bright color (such as red) in your borders can really liven up an otherwise dull sweater.

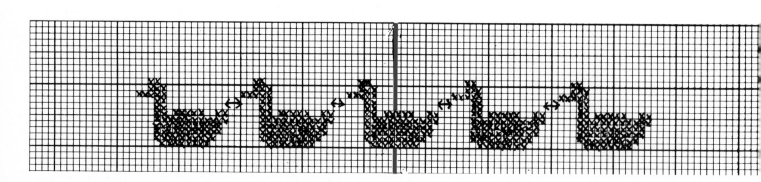

Centering and marking the first line of ducks on the graph.

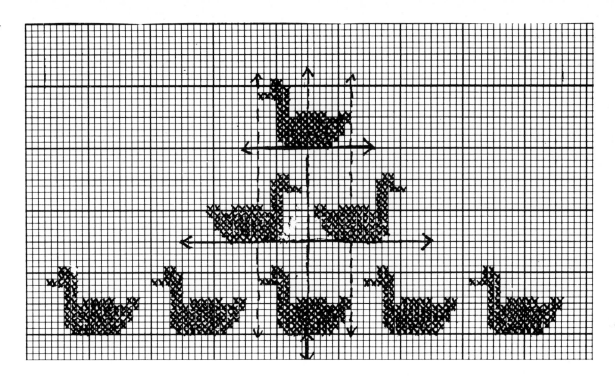

Finished graph of Sitting Ducks design.

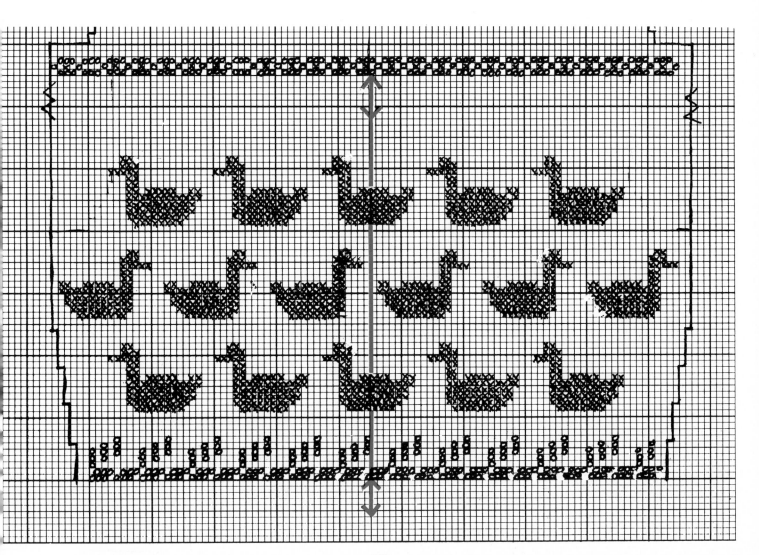

5.

"When you're knitting a sweater for someone, you think about how they'll look in the sweater . . . the expression of surprise on their face . . . and somehow all those thoughts become entwined in the sweater."

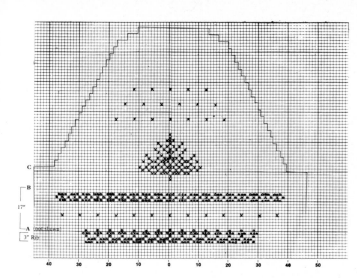

Sleeve pattern graph.

Picture Knit Country Cabin
Women's Size 34 - 36*

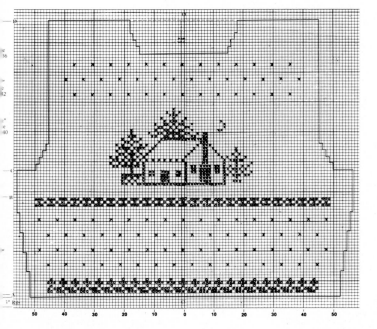

Body pattern graph.

Color Key:

Background -
Navy heather
x = Ecru
o = Cardinal red
Germantown by Brunswick

Machine knitters:
Use dot card; hand-pull
cabin and borders.

*For Women's Size 30 - 32
deduct 2 stitches from each
side of the sleeve and body
graphs.

*For Women's Size 38 - 40
add 2 stitches to each side of
the sleeve and body graphs.

Follow instructions on pages
12 and 13 for correct length.

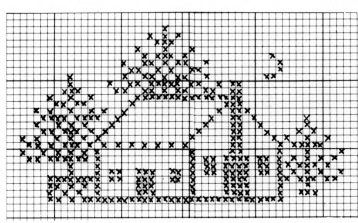

Detail of picture pattern.

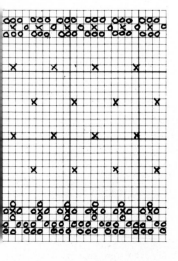

Detail of top border pattern.

Detail of dot pattern.

Detail of bottom border pattern.

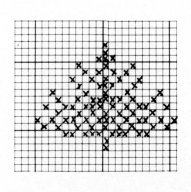

Detail of sleeve pattern.

31

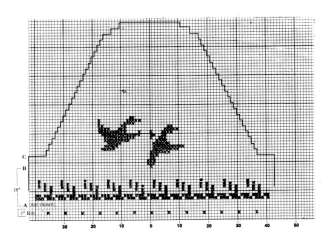

Sleeve pattern graph.

Picture Knit Hunting Dog
Men's Size 38 - 40★

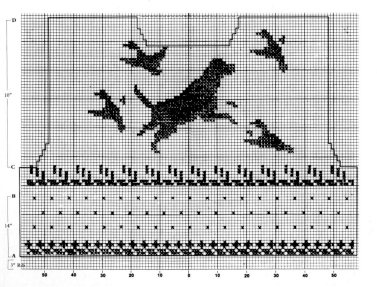

Body pattern graph.

Color Key:

Background -
Scotch heather and
Jade heather
x = Black
o = Scotch heather
■ = Jade heather
Germantown by Brunswick

Machine knitters:
Hand-pull borders and
picture pattern; use dot card.

★
For Men's Size 42 - 44
add 4 stitches to each side
of the body graph. Add 2
stitches to each side of the
sleeve graph.

★For Men's Size 46
add 8 stitches to each side
of the body graph. Add 2
stitches to each side of the
sleeve graph.

Follow instructions on pages
10 and 11 for correct length.

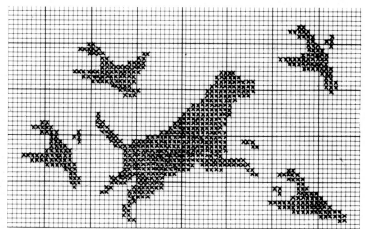

Detail of picture pattern.

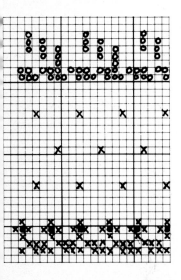

Detail of top border pattern.

Detail of dot pattern.

Detail of bottom border pattern.

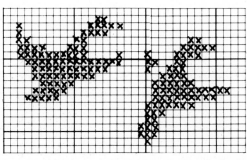

Detail of sleeve pattern.

Picture Knit Cows
Children's Size 10★

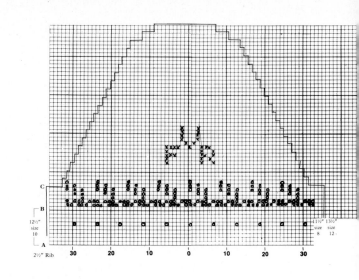

Sleeve pattern graph.

Color Key:

Background -
Cardinal red
x = White
. = Black
o = Dartmouth green

Germantown by Brunswick

Note: This cow pattern is
the most difficult in the
book. You may wish to
embroider over the black
after the piece is complete.

★**For Children's Size 8**
deduct 2 stitches from each
side of the graph.

★**For Children's Size 12**
add 2 stitches to each side of
the body graph.

Follow instructions on pages
13 and 14 for correct length.

Machine knitters:
Use dot card; hand-pull cows
and borders.

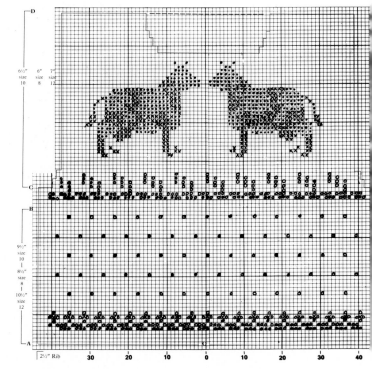

Body pattern graph.

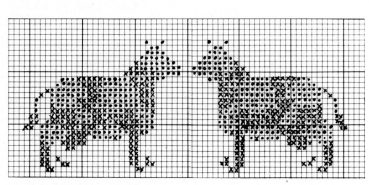

Detail of picture pattern.

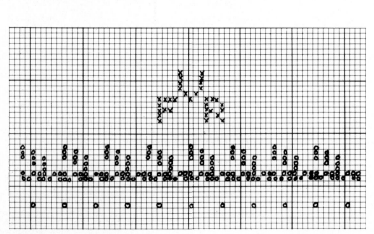

Detail of sleeve pattern.

Detail of top border pattern.

Detail of dot pattern.

Detail of bottom border pattern.

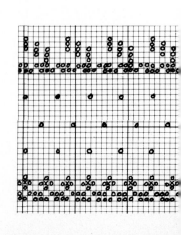

34

Picture Knit Scotties/Westies
Women's Size 34 - 36★

Color Key:
Background -
Surf heather
x = White
o = Navy heather
. = Cardinal red
■ = Black
(Embroider over after each piece is finished)
Germantown by Brunswick

Machine knitters:
Use Westie/Scottie and dot cards; hand-pull borders.

★**For Women's Size 30 - 32**
deduct 2 stitches from each side of the sleeve and body graphs.

★**For Women's Size 38 - 40**
add 2 stitches to each side of the sleeve and body graphs.

Follow instructions on pages 12 and 13 for correct length.

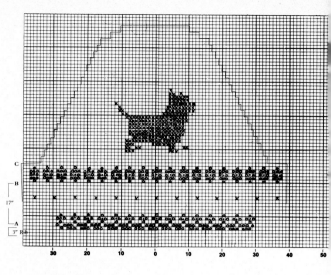

Sleeve pattern graph.

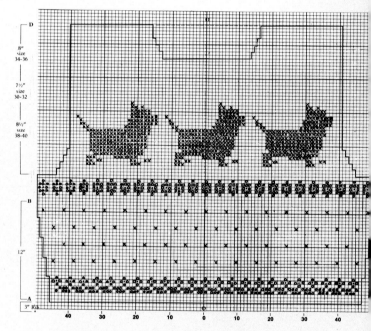

Body pattern graph.

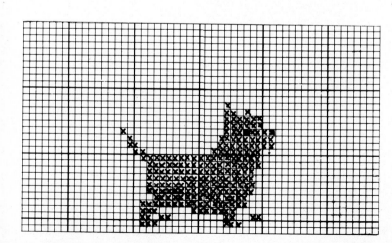

Detail of picture pattern.

Detail of top border pattern.

Detail of dot pattern.

Detail of bottom border pattern.

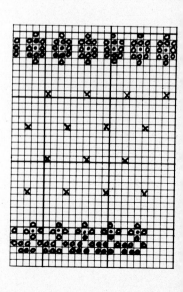

36

Picture Knit Victorian Stroller
Women's Size 34 - 36★

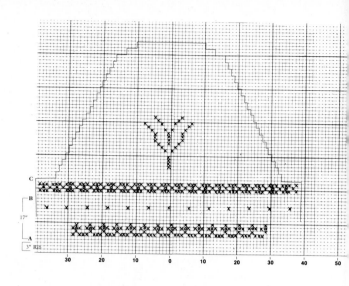

Sleeve pattern graph.

Color Key:

Background –
Scotch heather
x = Rosewood pink
o = Ecru

Germantown by Brunswick

Machine knitters:
Use Victorians strolling card
and dot card; hand-pull
borders.

★For Women's Size 30 - 32
deduct 2 stitches from each
side of the sleeve and body
graphs.

★For Women's Size 38 - 40
add 2 stitches to each side of
the sleeve and body graphs.

Follow instructions on pages
12 and 13 for correct length.

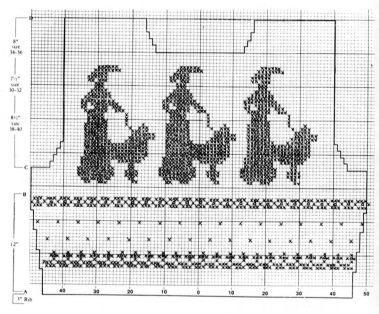

Body pattern graph.

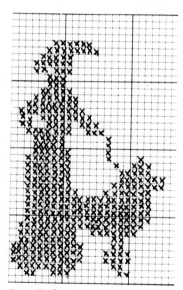

Detail of picture pattern.

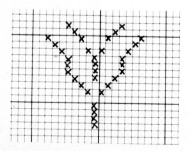

Detail of sleeve pattern.

Detail of top border pattern.

Detail of dot pattern.

Detail of bottom border pattern.

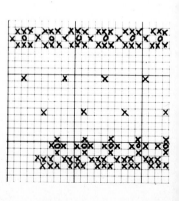

Picture Knit Sledding
Women's Size 34 - 36*

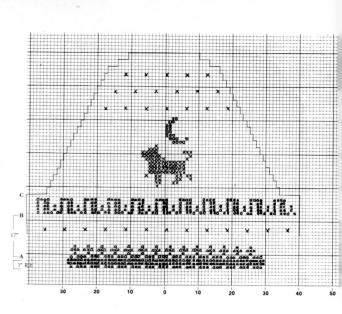

Sleeve pattern graph.

Color Key:

Background -
Cardinal red
x = Navy heather
o = Blue Ridge heather
Germantown by Brunswick

Embroider over moon after
each piece is finished.

Machine knitters:
Use dot card; hand-pull
picture patterns and borders.

*For Women's Size 30 - 32
deduct 2 stitches from each
side of the sleeve and body
graphs.

*For Women's Size 38 - 40
add 2 stitches to each side of
the sleeve and body graphs.

Follow instructions on pages
12 and 13 for correct length.

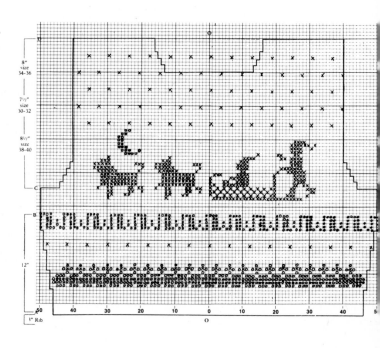

Body pattern graph.

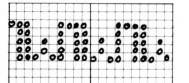

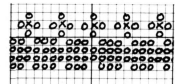

Detail of top border pattern.

Detail of bottom border pattern.

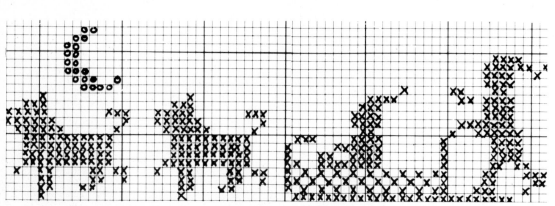

Detail of picture pattern.

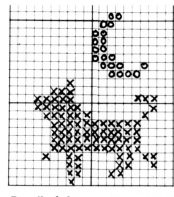

Detail of sleeve pattern.

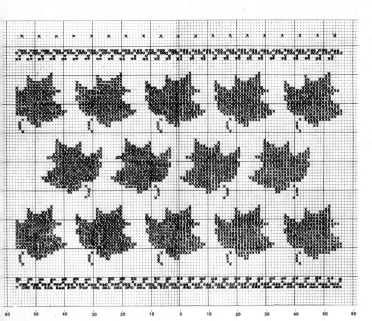

Body pattern graph.

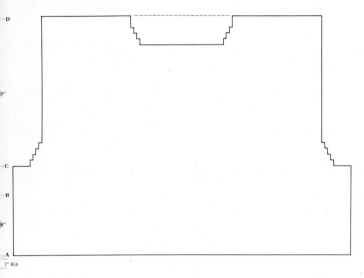

Picture Knit Maple Leaves
Men's Size 38 - 40★

Color Key:

Background -
Berber brown heather
x = Black
o = Jute heather
Germantown by Brunswick

Graph shows bottom of
sweater only.

Note: Follow standard
instructions but *do not* begin
underarm decrease in the 3rd
row above the top border
pattern. Instead, start
decrease when correct length
has been reached.

★

For Men's Size 42 - 44
add 4 stitches to each side
of the body graph. Add 2
stitches to each side of the
sleeve graph.

★For Men's Size 46
add 8 stitches to each side
of the body graph. Add 2
stitches to each side of the
sleeve graph.

Follow instructions on pages
10 and 11 for correct length.

Machine knitters:
Use maple leaf card for
bottom and dot card for top.
Hand-pull needles for
border.
Note: Maple leaf punch card
has 2 vertical repeats. After
2nd repeat has been knit,
knit 1 plain row, roll punch
card back to your start
position, and knit 3rd repeat.

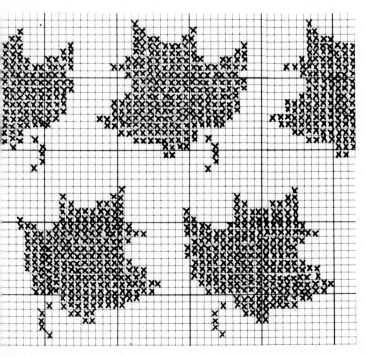

Detail of picture pattern.

Detail of top border pattern.

Detail of bottom border pattern.

43

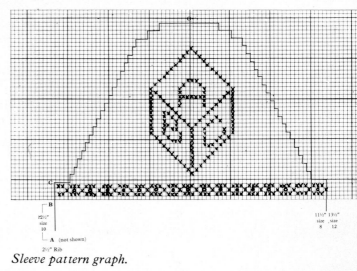

Sleeve pattern graph.

Picture Knit Teddy Bears
Children's Size 10*

Color Key:
Background -
Surf heather
x = Jute heather
o = Berber brown heather
■ = Black (for eyes)
Germantown by Brunswick

Machine knitters:
Hand-pull bears and
borders; use dot card.

★For Children's Size 8
deduct 2 stitches from each
side of the graph.
★For Children's Size 12
add 2 stitches to each side of
the body graph.

Follow instructions on pages
13 and 14 for correct length.

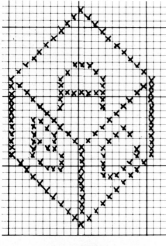

Detail of sleeve pattern.

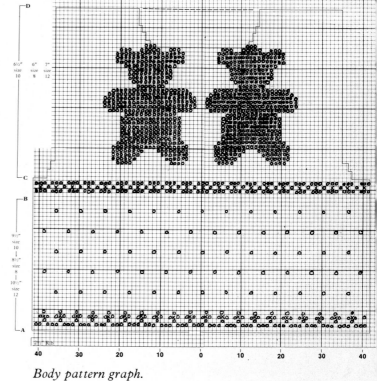

Body pattern graph.

Detail of top border pattern.

Detail of dot pattern.

Detail of bottom border pattern.

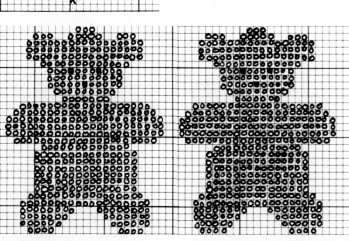

Detail of picture pattern.

44

Picture Knit Labrador
Women's Size 34 - 36★

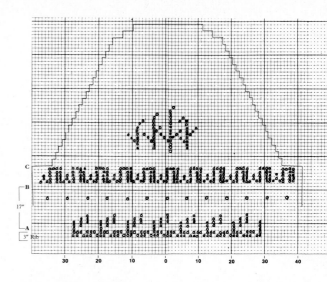

Sleeve pattern graph.

Color Key:

Background -
Camel (jute heather)
x = Black
o = Dartmouth green

Germantown by Brunswick

Machine knitters:
Use dot card and hand-pull dog and borders. Embroider over reeds when each piece is finished. Pattern will be reversed since you're working on the wrong side of the fabric.

★**For Women's Size 30 - 32** deduct 2 stitches from each side of the sleeve and body graphs.

★**For Women's Size 38 - 40** add 2 stitches to each side of the sleeve and body graphs.

Follow instructions on pages 12 and 13 for correct length.

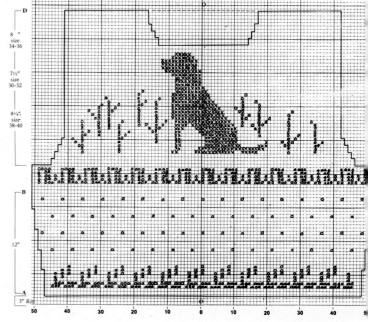

Body pattern graph.

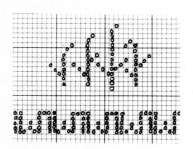

Detail of sleeve pattern.

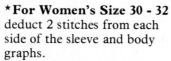

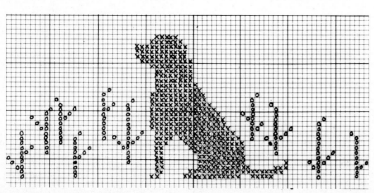

Detail of picture pattern.

Detail of top border pattern.

Detail of dot pattern.

Detail of bottom border pattern.

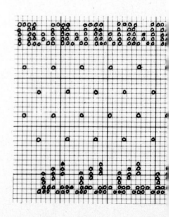

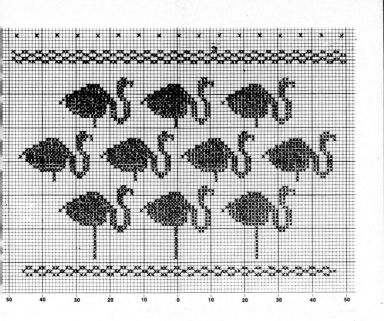

Body pattern graph.

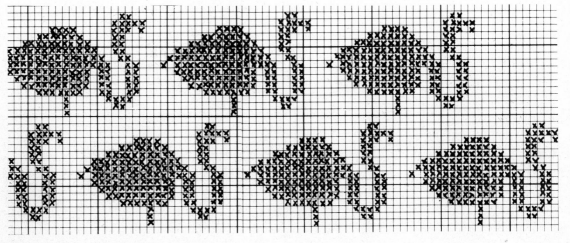

Color Key:

Background - 963 blue
x = 962 pink

Mayflower Cotton
Helarsgarn by Scheepjeswol

Note: For this sweater only, ignore **B** length measurement and measure length from beginning of rib to **C**.

★**For Women's Size 30 - 32** deduct 2 stitches from each side of the sleeve and body graphs.

★**For Women's Size 38 - 40** add 2 stitches to each side of the sleeve and body graphs.

Follow instructions on pages 12 and 13 for correct length.

Machine knitters:
Use flamingo and dot cards; hand-pull borders.

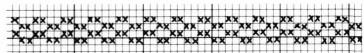

Detail of sleeve and body borders.

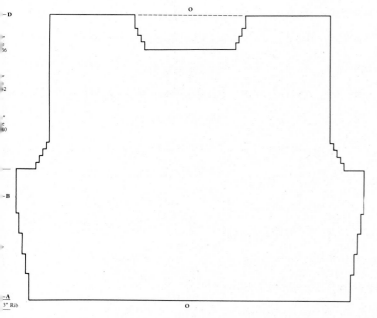

Detail of picture pattern.

Picture Knit Country Musicians
Men's Size 38 - 40★

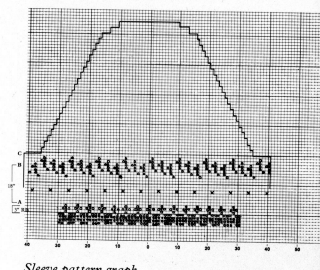

Sleeve pattern graph.

Color Key:

Background -
Navy heather
x = Cardinal red
o = Blue Ridge heather
Germantown by Brunswick

Embroider one moon when each piece is finished.

Machine knitters:
Use dot card; hand-pull picture pattern and borders. Refer to machine knitting directions for knitting with 3 colors.

★
For Men's Size 42 - 44
add 4 stitches to each side of the body graph. Add 2 stitches to each side of the sleeve graph.

★For Men's Size 46
add 8 stitches to each side of the body graph. Add 2 stitches to each side of the sleeve graph.

Follow instructions on pages 10 and 11 for correct length.

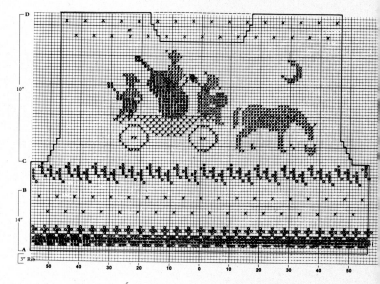

Body pattern graph.

Detail of picture pattern.

Detail of top border pattern.

Detail of dot pattern.

Detail of bottom border pattern.

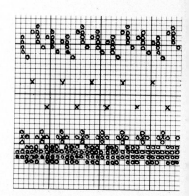

50

Picture Knit Elves *Children's Size 4*⋆

Color Key:

Background -
Dartmouth green
x = Ecru
o = Cardinal red
Germantown by Brunswick

Machine knitters:
Use dot card; hand-pull elves
and borders.

⋆**For Children's Size 2**
deduct 2 stitches from each
side of the body graph.

⋆**For Children's Size 6**
add 2 stitches to each side of
the body graph.

Follow instructions on pages
14 and 15 for correct length.

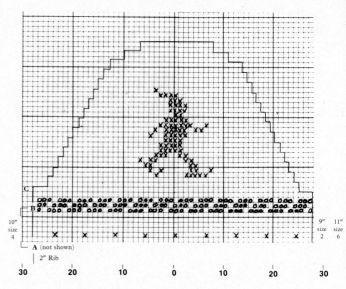

Sleeve pattern graph.

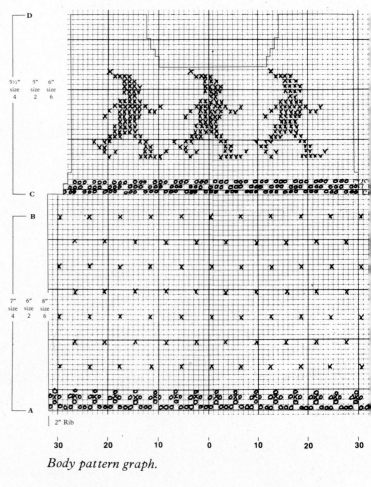

Body pattern graph.

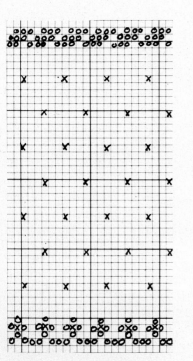

Detail of top border pattern.

Detail of dot pattern.

Detail of bottom border pattern.

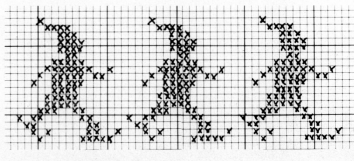

Detail of picture pattern.

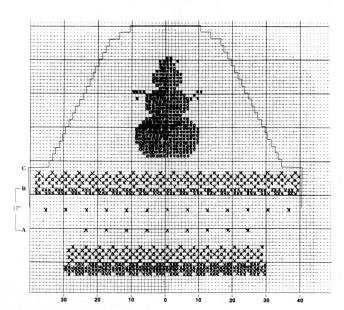

Sleeve pattern graph.

Picture Knit Snowmen
Women's Size 34 - 36★

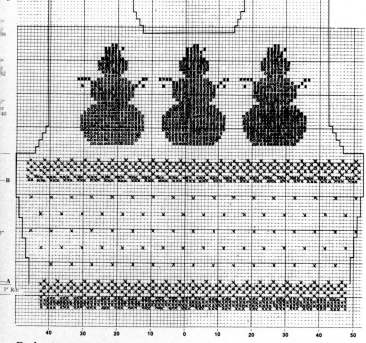

Body pattern graph.

Color Key:

Background -
Blue Ridge heather
x = Rosewood pink
o = Ecru
■ = Navy heather

Germantown by Brunswick

Note: Because borders are so large in this sweater, make the **A** to **B** body and sleeve length measurements 1″ shorter than specified.

★**For Women's Size 30 - 32** deduct 2 stitches from each side of the sleeve and body graphs.

★**For Women's Size 38 - 40** add 2 stitches to each side of the sleeve and body graphs.

Follow instructions on pages 12 and 13 for correct length.

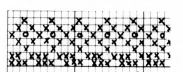

Detail of top border pattern.

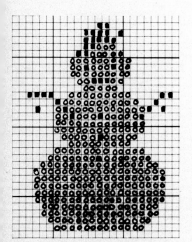

Detail of picture pattern.

Detail of dot pattern.

Detail of bottom border pattern.

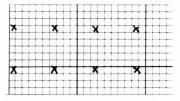

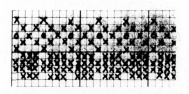

Picture Knit Newfie & Pups
Children's Size 4★

Color Key:

Background -
Cardinal red
x = Black
o = Cambridge heather
Germantown by Brunswick

Machine knitters:
Use dot card; hand-pull
picture pattern and borders.

★For Children's Size 2
deduct 2 stitches from each
side of the body graph.

★For Children's Size 6
add 2 stitches to each side of
the body graph.

Follow instructions on pages
14 and 15 for correct length.

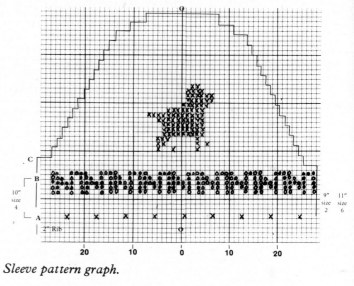

Sleeve pattern graph.

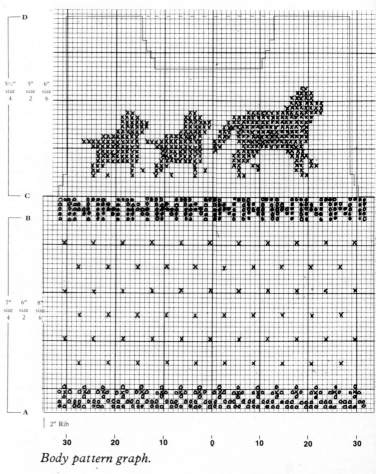

Body pattern graph.

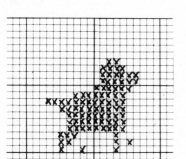

Detail of sleeve pattern.

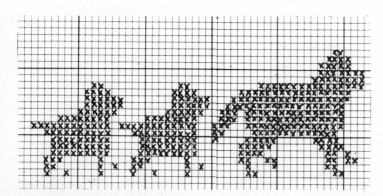

Detail of picture pattern.

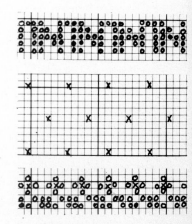

Detail of top border pattern.

Detail of dot pattern.

Detail of bottom border pattern.

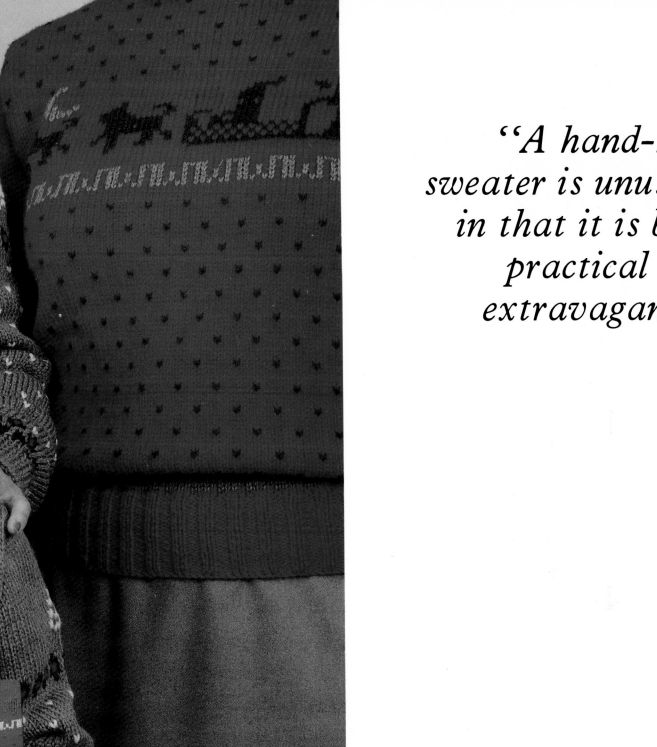

6.

"A hand-knit sweater is unusual in that it is both practical and extravagant."

Picture Knit Sitting Ducks
Children's Size 4★

Color Key:

Background -
Jute heather
x = Navy heather
o = Light blue jean heather
Germantown by Brunswick

Machine knitters:
Use duck and dot cards;
hand-pull borders.

★For Children's Size 2
deduct 2 stitches from each
side of the body graph.

★For Children's Size 6
add 2 stitches to each side of
the body graph.

Follow instructions on pages
14 and 15 for correct length.

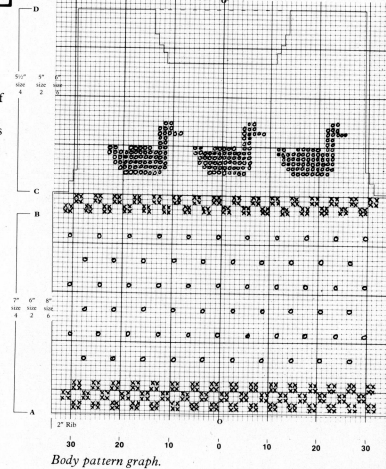

Sleeve pattern graph.

Body pattern graph.

Detail of top border pattern.

Detail of dot pattern.

Detail of bottom border pattern.

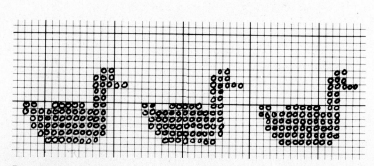

Detail of picture pattern.

60

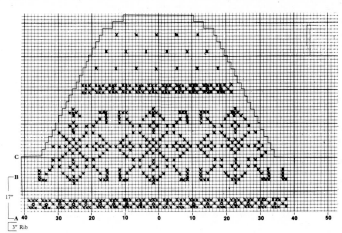

Sleeve pattern graph.

Picture Knit Snowflakes
Women's Size 34 - 36★

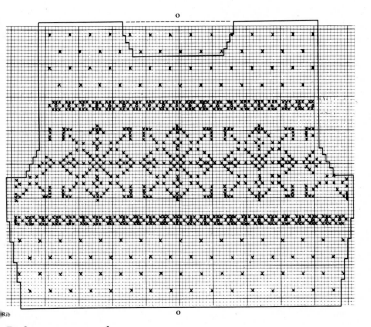

Body pattern graph.

Color Key:

Background -
Light blue jean heather
x = Ecru
o = Cardinal red
Germantown by Brunswick

Machine knitters:
Use snowflake and dot cards;
hand-pull borders.

★**For Women's Size 30 - 32**
deduct 2 stitches from each
side of the sleeve and body
graphs.

★**For Women's Size 38 - 40**
add 2 stitches to each side of
the sleeve and body graphs.

Follow instructions on pages
12 and 13 for correct length.

Detail of picture pattern.

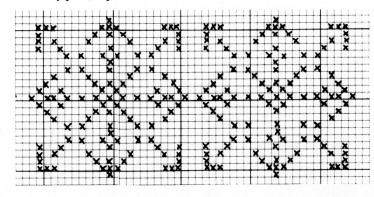

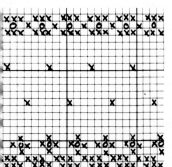

Detail of top border pattern.

Detail of dot pattern.

Detail of bottom border pattern.

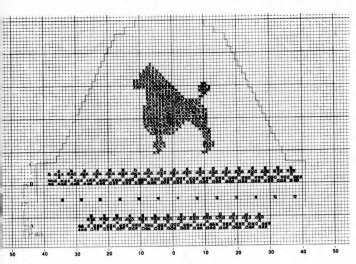

Sleeve pattern graph.

Picture Knit Poodles
Women's Size 34 - 36★

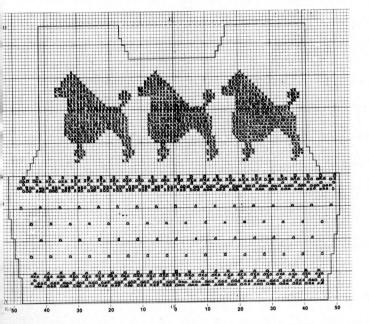

Color Key:

Background -
Rosewood pink
x = Ecru
o = Amethyst heather
Germantown by Brunswick

Machine knitters:
Use dot card on bottom;
hand-pull borders and
poodles.

★For Women's Size 30 - 32
deduct 2 stitches from each
side of the sleeve and body
graphs.

★For Women's Size 38 - 40
add 2 stitches to each side of
the sleeve and body graphs.

Follow instructions on pages
12 and 13 for correct length.

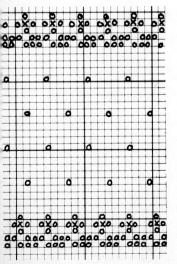

Detail of top border pattern.

Detail of dot pattern.

Detail of bottom border pattern.

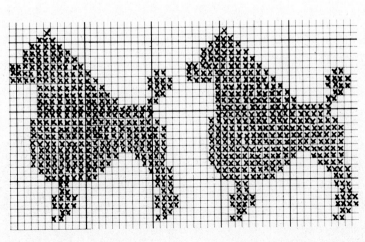

Detail of picture pattern.

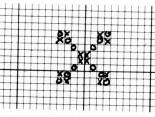

Picture Knit Horse & Sleigh
Children's Size 4★

Color Key:

Background –
Navy heather
o = Fuchsia
x = Ecru

Germantown by Brunswick

Color Key:

Background –
Periwinkle blue
o = Light pink
x = Ecru

Germantown by Brunswick

★For Children's Size 2
deduct 2 stitches from each
side of the body graph.

★For Children's Size 6
add 2 stitches to each side of
the body graph.

Follow instructions on pages
14 and 15 for correct length.

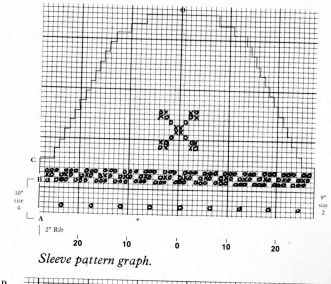

Sleeve pattern graph.

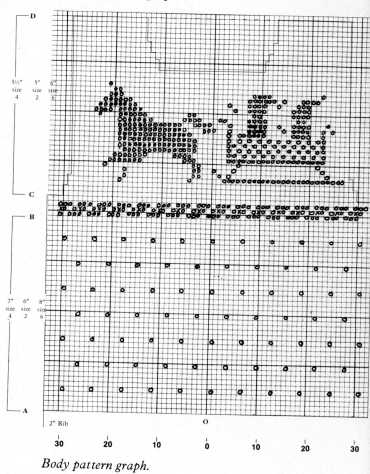

Body pattern graph.

Detail of sleeve pattern.

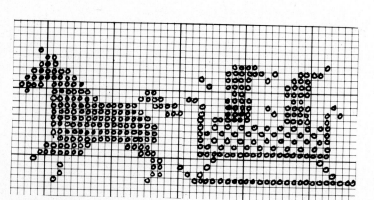

Detail of picture pattern.

Detail of top border pattern.

Detail of dot pattern.

Detail of bottom border pattern.

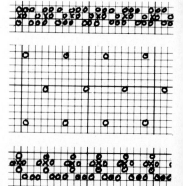

Picture Knit Elephant Children's Size 4★

Color Key:

Background - 920 green
x = 901 white

Mayflower Cotton
Helarsgarn by Scheepjeswol

Machine knitters:
Use dot card; hand-pull
elephant and borders.

★For Children's Size 2
deduct 2 stitches from each
side of the body graph.

★For Children's Size 6
add 2 stitches to each side of
the body graph.

Follow instructions on pages
14 and 15 for correct length.

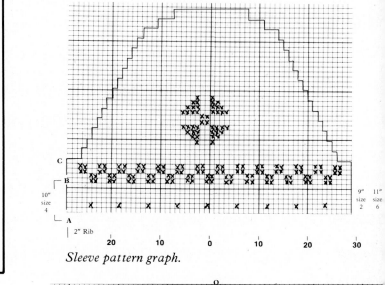

Sleeve pattern graph.

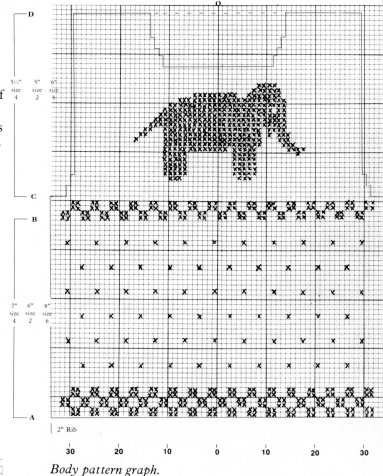

Body pattern graph.

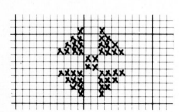

Detail of sleeve pattern.

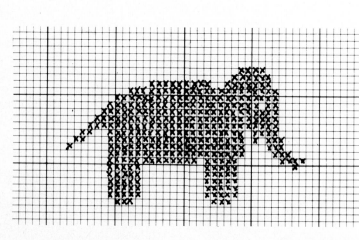

Detail of picture pattern.

Detail of dot pattern.

*Detail of sleeve and body
borders.*

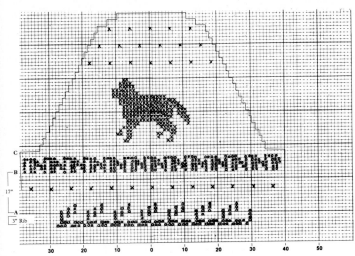

Sleeve pattern graph.

Picture Knit Newfoundlands
Women's Size 34 - 36*

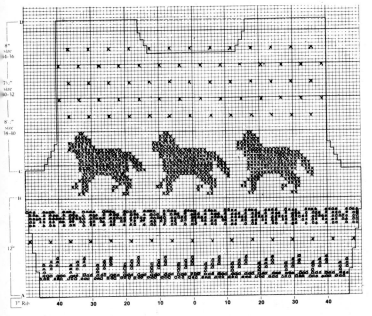

Sleeve pattern graph.

Color Key:

Background -
Camel (jute heather)
x = Black
o = Dartmouth green
Germantown by Brunswick

Machine knitters:
Use dot and Newfoundland
cards; hand-pull borders.

*For Women's Size 30 - 32
deduct 2 stitches from each
side of the sleeve and body
graphs.

*For Women's Size 38 - 40
add 2 stitches to each side of
the sleeve and body graphs.

Follow instructions on pages
12 and 13 for correct length.

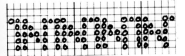

Detail of top border pattern.

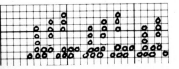

Detail of bottom border pattern.

Detail of dot pattern.

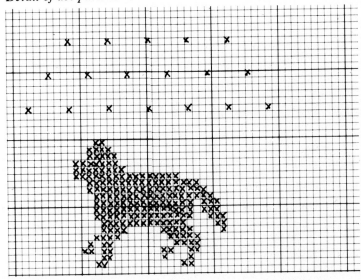

Detail of picture pattern.

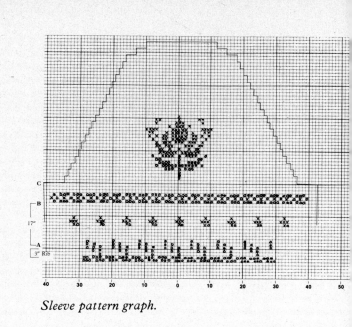

Sleeve pattern graph.

Picture Knit Roses
Women's Size 34 - 36★

Color Key:

Background - Ecru
x = Rosewood pink
o = Jade heather

Germantown by Brunswick

★For Women's Size 30 - 32 deduct 2 stitches from each side of the sleeve and body graphs.

★For Women's Size 38 - 40 add 2 stitches to each side of the sleeve and body graphs.

Follow instructions on pages 12 and 13 for correct length.

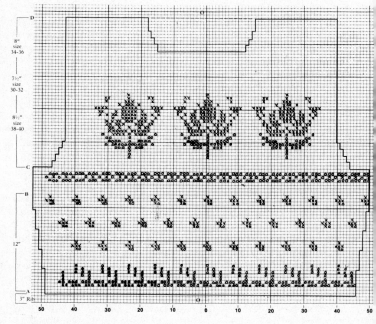

Body pattern graph.

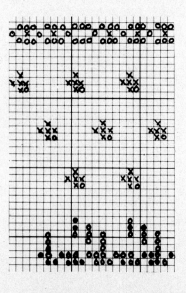

Detail of top border pattern.

Detail of dot pattern.

Detail of bottom border pattern.

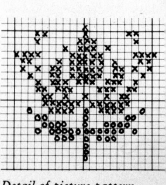

Detail of picture pattern.

Picture Knit Umbrella Ducks
Children's Size 4★

Color Key:
Background -
Cardinal red
x = Yellow
o = Navy heather
Germantown by Brunswick

★For Children's Size 2
deduct 2 stitches from each side of the body graph.

★For Children's Size 6
add 2 stitches to each side of the body graph.

Follow instructions on pages 14 and 15 for correct length.

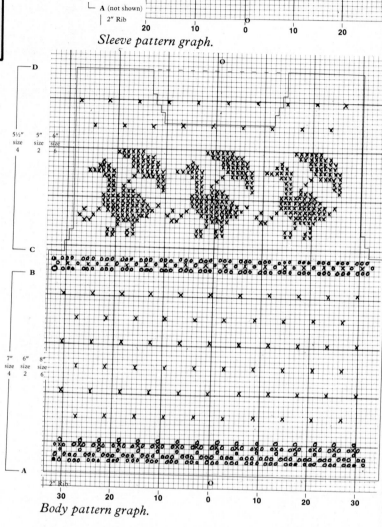

Sleeve pattern graph.

Body pattern graph.

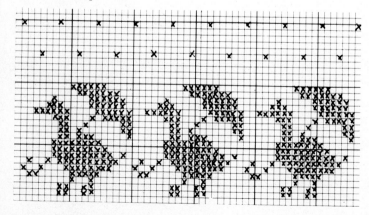

Detail of dot pattern.

Detail of picture pattern.

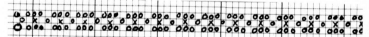

Detail of top border pattern.

Detail of bottom border pattern.

Body pattern graph.

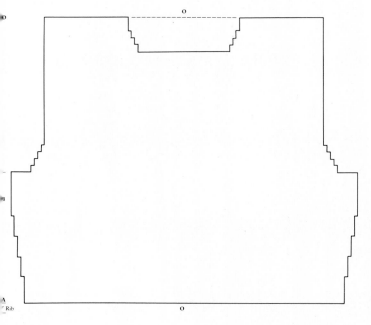

Picture Knit Tulips
Women's Size 34 - 36★

Detail of sleeve and body borders.

Color Key:

Background -
Amethyst heather
x = Plum heather
. = Rosewood pink
o = Scotch heather

Germantown by Brunswick

Note: Embroider over stems when each piece is finished.

★For Women's Size 30 - 32 deduct 2 stitches from each side of the sleeve and body graphs.

★For Women's Size 38 - 40 add 2 stitches to each side of the sleeve and body graphs.

Follow instructions on pages 12 and 13 for correct length.

Note: For this sweater only, do not begin underarm decrease at **B**. Begin underarm decrease at **C**.

Excellent for machine knitting. Use the tulip card for body. Switch yarn color from plum heather to rosewood pink after first group of tulips, then back to plum heather after second group. Use dot card for top of sweater. Hand-pull borders.

After 2nd repeat of tulips, knit 1 plain row, then roll tulip card back to start. Now knit 3rd repeat of tulips.

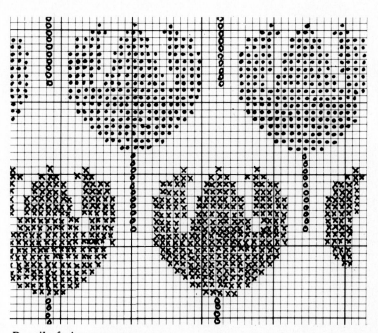

Detail of picture pattern.

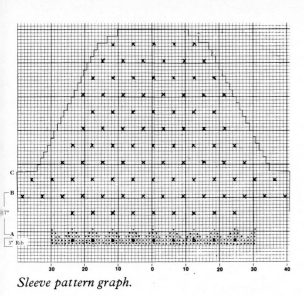

Sleeve pattern graph.

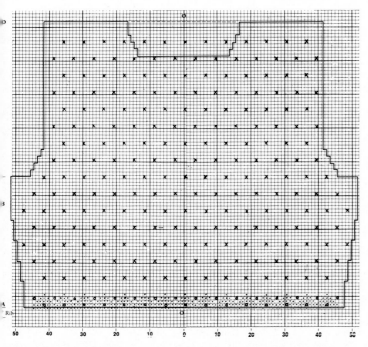

Body pattern graph.

Color Key:

Background -
Cambridge heather (gray)
x = Ecru
o = Cardinal red
. = Black
(make ribbings in black also)

Germantown by Brunswick

Note: For this sweater only, there is no top border

★**For Women's Size 30 - 32** deduct 2 stitches from each side of the sleeve and body graphs.

★**For Women's Size 38 - 40** add 2 stitches to each side of the sleeve and body graphs.

Follow instructions on pages 12 and 13 for correct length.

Machine knitters:
Use dot card; hand-pull borders.

Detail of dot pattern.

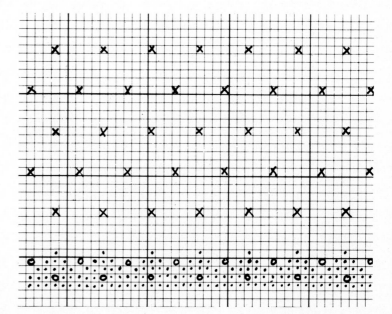

Detail of bottom border pattern.

Picture Knit Palm Trees
Children's Size 10*

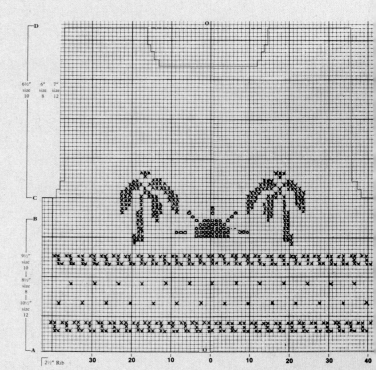

Sleeve pattern graph.

Color Key:

Background - 901 white
x = 920 green
o = 903 orange

Mayflower Cotton
Helarsgarn by Scheepjeswol

Machine knitters:
Use dot card; hand-pull
picture pattern and borders.

*For Children's Size 8
deduct 2 stitches from each
side of the graph.

*For Children's Size 12
add 2 stitches to each side of
the body graph.

Follow instructions on pages
13 and 14 for correct length.

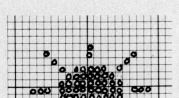

Detail of sleeve pattern.

Body pattern graph.

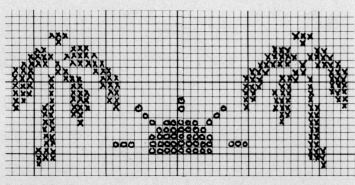

Detail of picture pattern.

*Detail of sleeve and body
borders.*

Detail of dot pattern.

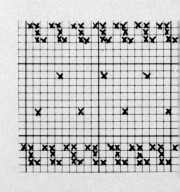

Picture Knit Lambs
Children's Size 10*

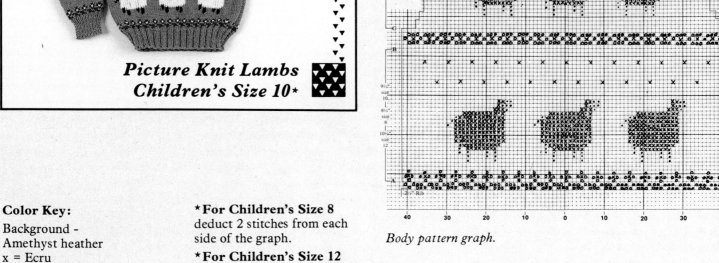

Body pattern graph.

Color Key:

Background -
Amethyst heather
x = Ecru
o = Plum heather
  = Black
(embroider one after each
piece is finished)

Germantown by Brunswick

Machine knitters:
Use lamb card and dot card;
hand-pull borders; lambs will
be reversed.

*For Children's Size 8
deduct 2 stitches from each
side of the graph.

*For Children's Size 12
add 2 stitches to each side of
the body graph.

Follow instructions on pages
13 and 14 for correct length.

Detail of top border pattern.

Detail of picture pattern.

Detail of bottom border pattern.

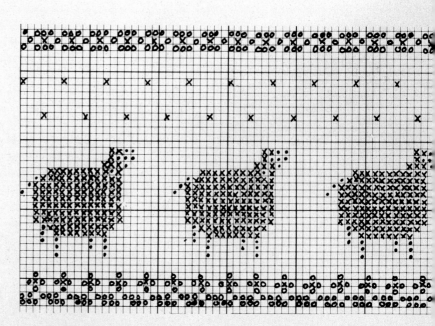

Picture Knit Reindeer
Men's Size 38 - 40★

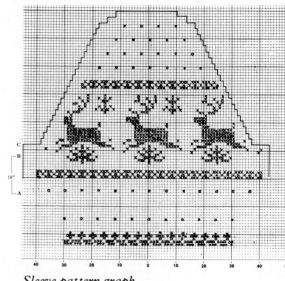

Sleeve pattern graph.

Color Key:

Background -
Blue Ridge heather and
Navy heather
x = White
o = Navy heather

Germantown by Brunswick

Note: For this pattern only,
begin reindeer border when
work measures 15 inches
from the beginning of the
rib. Begin the underarm
decrease when work
measures 17 inches from the
beginning of the rib.

★

For Men's Size 42 - 44
add 4 stitches to each side
of the body graph. Add 2
stitches to each side of the
sleeve graph.

★For Men's Size 46
add 8 stitches to each side
of the body graph. Add 2
stitches to each side of the
sleeve graph.

Follow instructions on pages
10 and 11 for correct length.

Machine knitters:
This pattern is excellent for
machine knitting. There's no
hand-pulling of needles except for the bottom border.
Use dot card for above and
below reindeer borders; use
reindeer card with borders.

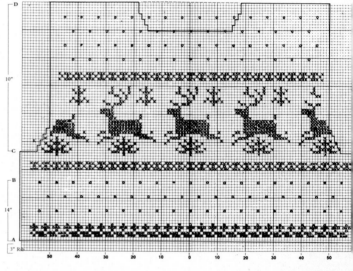

Body pattern graph.

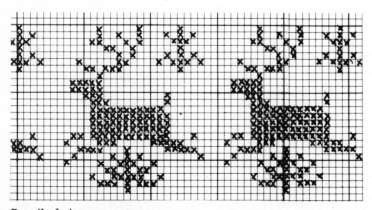

Detail of picture pattern.

Detail of top border pattern.

Detail of dot pattern.

Detail of bottom border pattern.

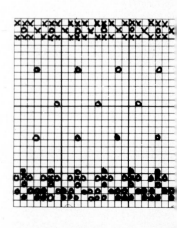

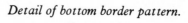

February 22, 1988:
Jonathon's 9th birthday.

↑ "I'm going to be famous, really?"

↑ Is he cute or what?

↑ "When
Shades

↓ Aunt Mildred with Uncle
Ed's competition.

...ght she
...a hat
...er sweater!
...surprising
...poodle hair
...pit bull.

...she
...all summer?

↓ St. Valentine's Day, 1982

Cool-Dude
...ed them?"

7

"To make a sweater for someone is to knit together the past and the future into a gift of warmth."

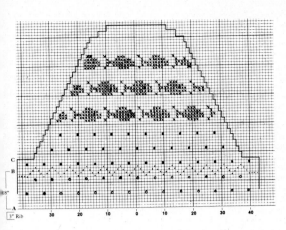

Sleeve pattern graph.

Picture Knit Fish
Men's Size 38 - 40★

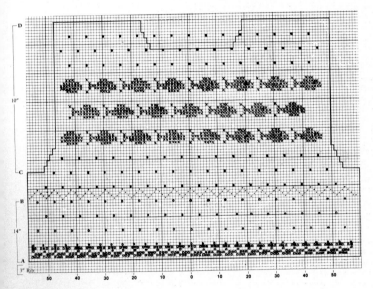

Body pattern graph.

Color Key:

Bottom background -
Dartmouth green
Top background -
Jade heather
■ = Ecru
x = Dartmouth green
o = Jade heather

Germantown by Brunswick

shows last row of
Dartmouth green
before background
color change

Machine knitters:
Use fish and dot cards;
hand-pull borders. hand-pull
eyes to HOLD position; knit
across row and then lay ecru
yarn over H needles. Push H
needles back to W by hand.
(See machine knitting
instructions.)

★
For Men's Size 42 - 44
add 4 stitches to each side
of the body graph. Add 2
stitches to each side of the
sleeve graph.

★For Men's Size 46
add 8 stitches to each side
of the body graph. Add 2
stitches to each side of the
sleeve graph.

Follow instructions on pages
10 and 11 for correct length.

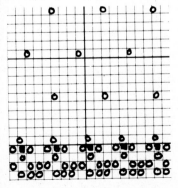

Detail of dot pattern.

Detail of sleeve and body borders.

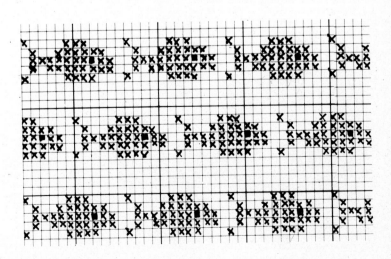

Detail of picture pattern.

Picture Knit Bunnies
Children's Size 4*

Color Key:

Background –
Light blue jean heather
x = Ecru
o = Navy heather

Germantown by Brunswick

Machine knitters:
Use bunny and dot cards;
hand-pull borders.

*For Children's Size 2
deduct 2 stitches from each
side of the body graph.

*For Children's Size 6
add 2 stitches to each side of
the body graph.

Follow instructions on pages
14 and 15 for correct length.

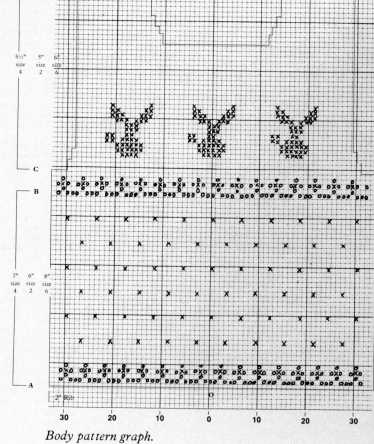

Sleeve pattern graph.

Body pattern graph.

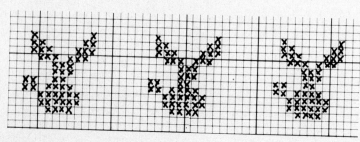

Detail of picture pattern.

Detail of dot pattern.

Detail of sleeve and body
borders.

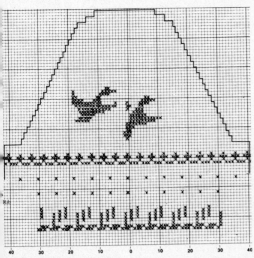

Sleeve pattern graph.

Picture Knit Flying Geese
Men's Size 38 - 40★

Color Key:

Background -
Cambridge Heather
x = Black
o = Dartmouth green
Germantown by Brunswick

★
For Men's Size 42 - 44
add 4 stitches to each side
of the body graph. Add 2
stitches to each side of the
sleeve graph.

★For Men's Size 46
add 8 stitches to each side
of the body graph. Add 2
stitches to each side of the
sleeve graph.

Follow instructions on pages
10 and 11 for correct length.

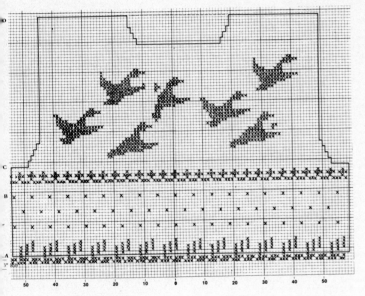

Body pattern graph.

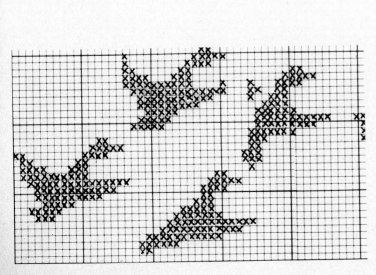

Detail of picture pattern.

Detail of top border pattern.

Detail of dot pattern.

Detail of bottom border pattern.

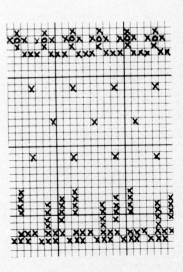

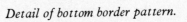

Picture Knit Sheep Dogs
Women's Size 34 - 36*

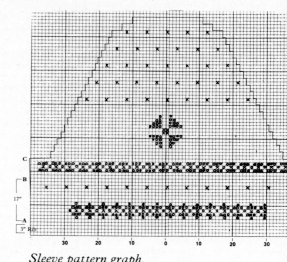

Sleeve pattern graph.

Color Key:

Background -
Surf heather
x = Ecru
o = Navy heather
. = Gray
■ = Black
(embroider over after each
piece is finished)
Germantown by Brunswick

Machine knitters:
Use dot card and hand-pull
picture pattern and borders.

*For Women's Size 30 - 32
deduct 2 stitches from each
side of the sleeve and body
graphs.

*For Women's Size 38 - 40
add 2 stitches to each side of
the sleeve and body graphs.

Follow instructions on pages
12 and 13 for correct length.

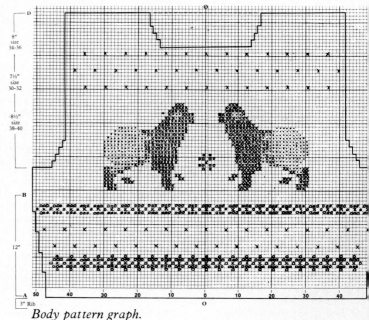

Body pattern graph.

Detail of sleeve pattern.

Detail of top border pattern.

Detail of dot pattern.

Detail of bottom border pattern.

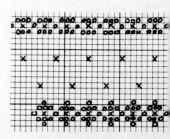

Detail of picture pattern.

94

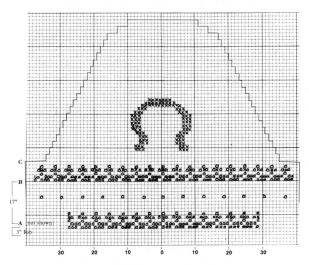

Sleeve pattern graph.

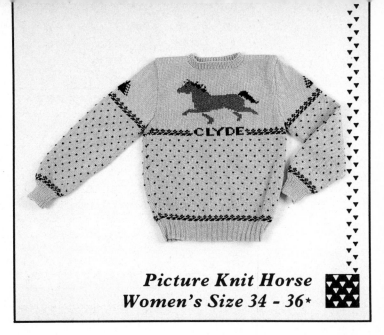

Picture Knit Horse
Women's Size 34 - 36★

Color Key:

Background -
Camel (jute heather)
x = Berber brown heather
o = Black
• = Black
(embroider over after piece is finished)
Germantown by Brunswick

Machine knitters:
Hand-pull horse and borders; use dot card for body of horse.

★**For Women's Size 30 - 32** deduct 2 stitches from each side of the sleeve and body graphs.

★**For Women's Size 38 - 40** add 2 stitches to each side of the sleeve and body graphs.

Follow instructions on pages 12 and 13 for correct length.

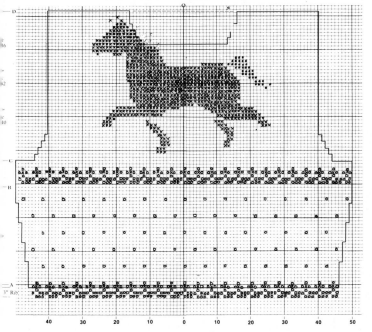

Body pattern graph.

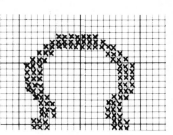

Detail of sleeve pattern.

Detail of top border pattern.

Detail of dot pattern.

Detail of bottom border pattern.

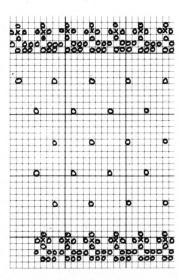

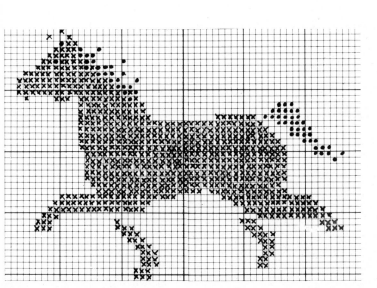

Detail of picture pattern.

Body pattern graph.

Picture Knit Piney Woods
Men's Size 34 - 36★

Color Key:

Background -
Dartmouth green
x = Ecru
o = Cardinal red

Germantown by Brunswick

★
For Men's Size 42 - 44
add 4 stitches to each side
of the body graph. Add 2
stitches to each side of the
sleeve graph.

★For Men's Size 46
add 8 stitches to each side
of the body graph. Add 2
stitches to each side of the
sleeve graph.

Follow instructions on pages
10 and 11 for correct length.

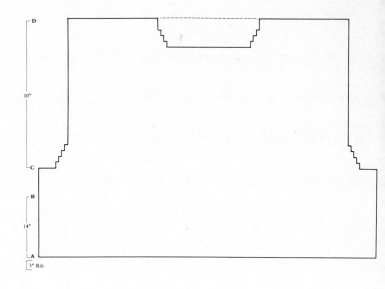

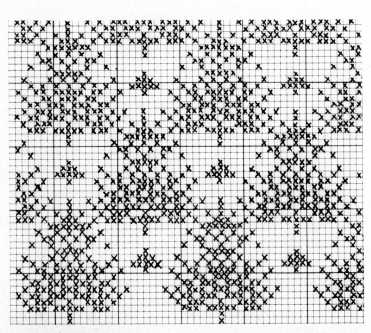

Detail of picture pattern.

Detail of top border pattern.

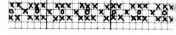

Detail of bottom border pattern.

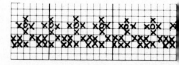

Picture Knit Winter Fun
Children's Size 4*

Color Key:

Background -
Navy heather
x = Cardinal red
o = Blue Ridge heather
Germantown by Brunswick

Machine knitters:
Use dot card; hand-pull
borders and picture pattern.

*For Children's Size 2
deduct 2 stitches from each
side of the body graph.

*For Children's Size 6
add 2 stitches to each side of
the body graph.

Follow instructions on pages
14 and 15 for correct length.

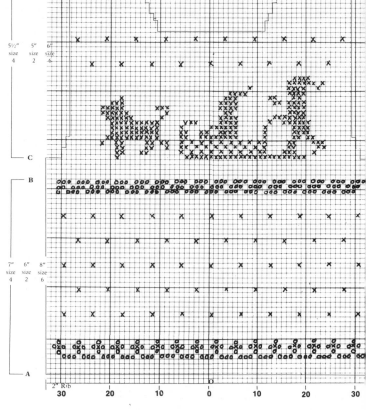

Sleeve pattern graph.

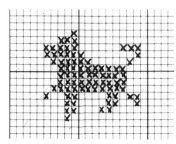

Detail of sleeve pattern.

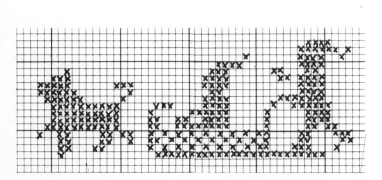

Detail of picture pattern.

Detail of top border pattern.

Detail of dot pattern.

Detail of bottom border pattern.

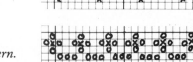

Picture Knit Tap Dancers
Women's Size 34 - 36*

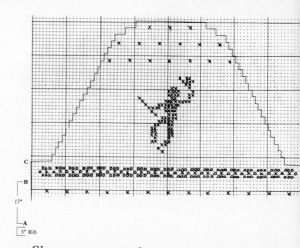

Sleeve pattern graph.

Color Key:

Background -
Plum heather
x = Ecru
o = Amethyst heather
Germantown by Brunswick

*For Women's Size 30 - 32 deduct 2 stitches from each side of the sleeve and body graphs.

*For Women's Size 38 - 40 add 2 stitches to each side of the sleeve and body graphs.

Follow instructions on pages 12 and 13 for correct length.

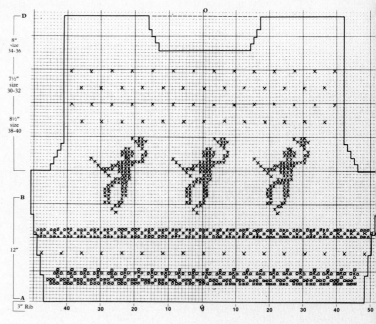

Body pattern graph.

Detail of dot pattern.

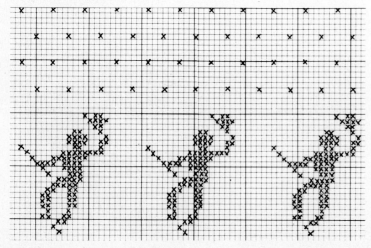

Detail of picture pattern.

Detail of top border pattern.

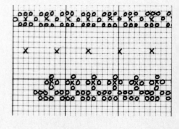

Detail of bottom border pattern.

Picture Knit Skiers
Men's Size 38 - 40★

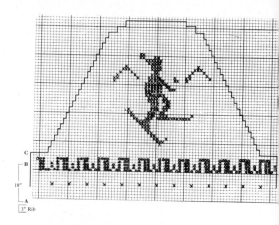

Sleeve pattern graph.

Color Key:

Background -
Dartmouth green
x = Ecru
o = Cardinal red

Germantown by Brunswick

★
For Men's Size 42 - 44
add 4 stitches to each side
of the body graph. Add 2
stitches to each side of the
sleeve graph.

★**For Men's Size 46**
add 8 stitches to each side
of the body graph. Add 2
stitches to each side of the
sleeve graph.

Follow instructions on pages
10 and 11 for correct length.

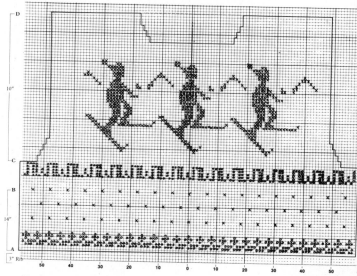

Body pattern graph.

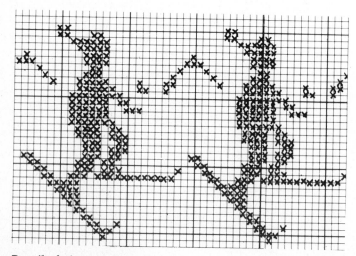

Detail of picture pattern.

Detail of top border pattern.

Detail of dot pattern.

Detail of bottom border pattern.

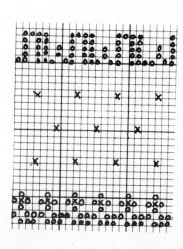

Picture Knit Christmas Cactus Children's Size 10★

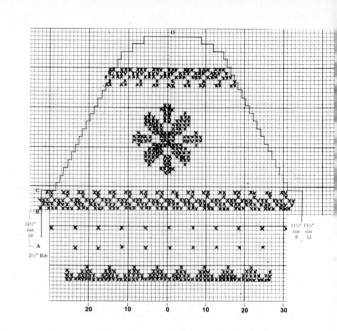

Color Key:

Background -
Periwinkle blue
Ribs = Scotch heather
+ last 2 rows of neck rib
x = Scotch heather

Germantown by Brunswick

Machine knitters:
This is a very easy pattern.
Use dot and cactus cards.

★For Children's Size 8
deduct 2 stitches from each
side of the graph.

★For Children's Size 12
add 2 stitches to each side of
the body graph.

Follow instructions on pages
13 and 14 for correct length.

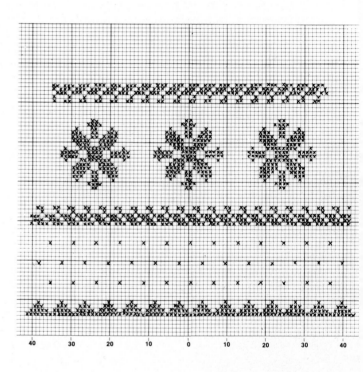

*Directions for girl's picture knit sweater
dress begin on page 116.*

Detail of top border pattern.

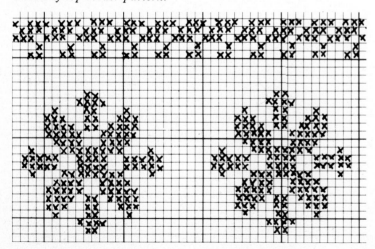

Detail of picture pattern.

*Detail of sleeve and body
borders.*

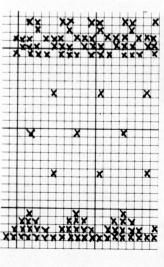

Picture Knit Cat Vest
Men's Size 38 - 40*

Directions for men's picture knit sweater vest begin on page 116.

Body pattern graph.

Color Key:

Background -
Berber brown heather
x = Ecru
o = Black
■ = Black - for nose
. = Surf heather - for eyes
o = Jute heather - for accent
    on cat
(embroider over when each
piece is finished)
Germantown by Brunswick

Machine knitters:
Use dot card; hand-pull cats
and borders.

*
For Men's Size 42 - 44
add 4 stitches to each side
of the body graph. Add 2
stitches to each side of the
sleeve graph.

★For Men's Size 46
add 8 stitches to each side
of the body graph. Add 2
stitches to each side of the
sleeve graph.

Follow instructions on pages
10 and 11 for correct length.

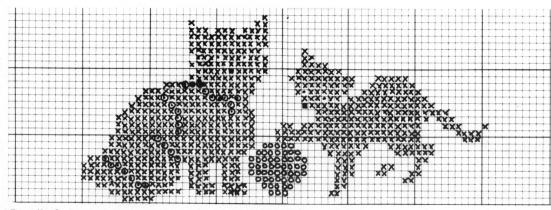

Detail of picture pattern.

108

Picture Knit ABC Baby Bag
Infant's Size 6 months to 1 year

Directions for infant's picture knit baby bag begin on page 114.

Color Key:

Background -
Navy heather
x = Cardinal red
o = Yellow

Germantown by Brunswick

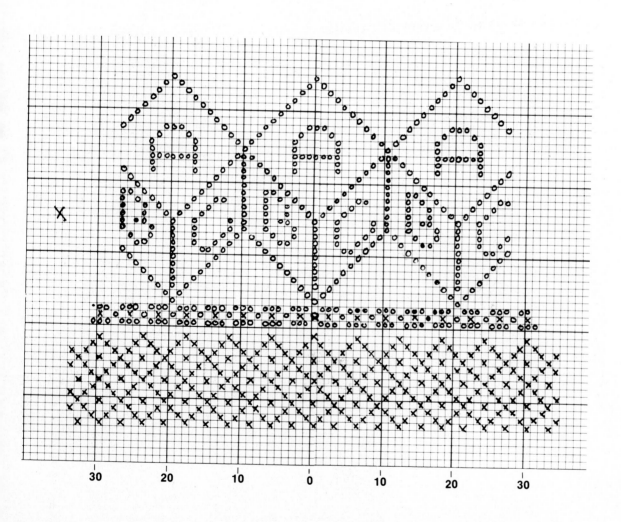

Picture Knit Little Maids
Baby Bag
Infant Size 6 months to 1 year

Color Key:
Background - Ecru
x = Fuchsia
o = Dartmouth green
Germantown by Brunswick

Machine knitters:
Use little maid and rosebud
cards; hand-pull borders.
Pattern will be reversed.

Directions for infant's picture knit baby bag begin on page 114.

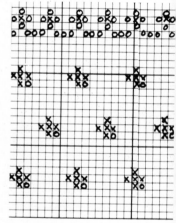

Detail of rosebuds and body border.

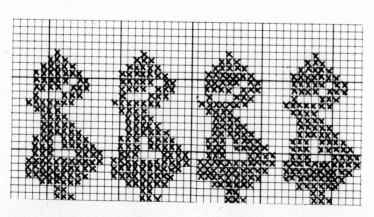

Detail of picture pattern.

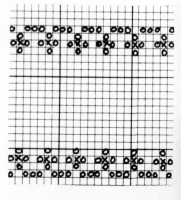

Detail of hood borders.

8.

Additional Projects

Baby Bag, Sweater Vest, Children's Sweater Dress, Mittens

Picture Knit Baby Bag

Size 6 months to 1 year

□ **Materials**

1 pair size 2 needles
1 pair size 5 needles
1 set (4) size 2 double-pointed needles
3 stitch holders
1 tapestry needle
1 zipper, 22 inches long
needle and thread to match background yarn

□ **Yarn**

   Amount of Germantown wool yarn needed*:
Background color — 4 skeins (14 oz; 400 gms).
Picture pattern color — 1 skein (3.5 oz; 100 gms).
Third color** — 1 small ball (1 oz; 28 gms).
   Amount of Helarsgarn cotton yarn needed*:
Background color — 10 skeins (500 gms; 17.5 oz).
Picture pattern color — 2 skeins (100 gms; 3.5 oz).
Third color** — 1 skein (50 gms; 1.75 oz).

* Since the weight of a skein varies from brand to brand, be
  sure to check the weight if you substitute yarns.

** Many of the sweaters in this book do not use a third color,
   so check the pattern graph before purchasing yarns.

□ **Gauge**

5½ stitches per inch. Measure your gauge at least 1 inch
below your needle.

□ **Stitches**

Key to stitches: k = knit; p = purl.

Ribbing Stitch: For front and back pieces, k2, p2; for sleeves
and neck, k1, p1.

Stockinette Stitch: Alternate rows of knit (right side) and
purl (wrong side).

Moss Stitch: k1, p1 the first row; thereafter, knit the purl
stitches and purl the knit stitches.

□ **Front**

(**Note:** The bag zips up the back so make the front first.)
   Using size 5 needles, cast on 73 stitches and work 4 plain
rows in a stockinette stitch. Begin following the pattern
diagram in the 5th row and continue knitting until the bag
measures 21 inches from the start.
   Work 4 plain rows and then knit the top border pattern.
Work 2 more plain rows. Then begin the underarm decrease
by binding off 4 stitches at the beginning of each of the next
2 rows. Follow the pattern graph and continue decreasing for
the underarm by binding off 1 stitch at the beginning of each
of the next 6 rows. 59 stitches should now remain.
   When the work measures 5½ inches up from the underarm
(measuring from the center of the work), begin decreasing for
the front neck opening as follows: Work 20 stitches. Slip the
next 19 stitches on a stitch holder (for the front neck
opening), and slip the remaining 20 stitches on a second
stitch holder. Work each side of the neck opening separately.
Decrease 1 stitch at the neck edge (every other row) three
times. Work the side until it measures 7 inches up from the
underarm decrease. Bind off the remaining 17 stitches.
Repeat with the other side of the neck opening.

Back

Work the same as the front until the piece measures 10 inches from the beginning.

Now work 37 stitches (for the right side of the back) and slip the remaining 36 stitches on a stitch holder. Work each side of the back separately.

Working the Right Side

Work the right side until the bag measures 21 inches from the beginning. Work 4 plain rows and then the top border pattern. Work 2 plain rows and begin decreasing for the underarm by binding off 4 stitches at the beginning of the next **outside edge** row. Continue decreasing for the underarm, following the graph, by binding off 1 stitch from the outside edge (every other row) 3 times. 30 stitches now remain.

When the back measures 7 inches up from the underarm, (measuring straight up from the center of the work), the right side is finished. Bind off 17 stitches from the outside edge and slip the remaining 13 stitches on a stitch holder for the back neck opening.

Working the Left Side

Pick up the 36 stitches for the left side and work the same as the right side. **Note:** Since there is one less stitch on this side, bind off 17 stitches at the end and place the remaining 12 stitches on a stitch holder for the back neck opening.

Arms

Using size 2 double-pointed needles, cast on 19 stitches and work in a rib of k1 p1 for 1½ inches. Then increase by casting on 18 more stitches at the end of your work, and continue working the rib until it measures 2½ inches from the beginning. 37 stitches will remain. When finished, the rib folds over itself to cover baby's hand.

Switch to size 5 needles and knit 1 plain row, increasing to 51 stitches in this first row by knitting the front and back of about every third stitch. Purl back and begin following the pattern diagram. When the work measures 7 inches up from the beginning of the rib, work the top border pattern. Then work 2 plain rows, and begin the underarm decrease by binding off 4 stitches from the beginning of each of the next 2 rows. Shape the top of the sleeve by binding off 1 stitch at the beginning of each row until 23 stitches remain. Bind off 3 stitches at the beginning of each of the next 4 rows. Bind off the remaining 11 stitches.

Assembling the Pieces

Assemble pieces for the body before making the hood. Don't sew the back seam at this time.

Sew the front and back together at shoulder seams. Then sew the bag's bottom seam. Sew side seams, arm seams and sew arms into body.

Making the Hood

Using size 2 straight needles, pick up and knit 64 stitches across the neck opening (13 from the right back opening, 10 from left front neck, 19 from front stitch holder, 10 from right front neck, and 12 from left back neck). Work in a rib of k1, p1 for 4 rows.

Now switch to size 5 needles and work the first 23 stitches.

Slip the next 19 stitches on a stitch holder (for the front neck), and slip the next 22 stitches on a stitch holder for the other side of the hood. It doesn't matter which side you work first.

The hood is worked in one piece and then attached to the other side of the neck. Work the first 23 stitches. Increase in the next row to 39 stitches by knitting the front and back of about every other stitch. Work 2 more plain rows, then begin the border pattern, following the pattern diagram. When the work measures 16½ inches from the beginning of the border pattern, work 4 plain rows, then the next border pattern, and then 3 plain rows.

Slip the 22 stitches from the other side of the neck onto a size 2 knitting needle. Working with right sides together, bind off the 22 stitches from the neck and the 39 stitches from the hood. Bind off about 2 stitches from the hood with every 1 stitch from the neck.

Front Hood Ribbing

Using size 2 double-pointed needles, pick up and knit 74 stitches around the front hood opening for the rib (19 from the front stitch holder and 55 from around the front edge of the hood).

Work the stitches in a rib of k1, p1 (match the front neck ribbing) for 5 rows. Bind off loosely.

The Back Opening

Pick up 83 stitches on the right edge of the back opening — from the bottom of the opening up through about 3 inches into the hood. Work in a moss stitch for 3 rows. Bind off loosely. Repeat for the opposite side of the back.

Sewing the Zipper

With the bag right side out, lay the zipper on top of the moss stitches on the left side of the opening. Sew in place with needle and thread. Then place the moss stitches from the right side of the opening on top of the zipper and sew in the right side of the zipper.

With a tapestry needle and matching yarn, sew the bottom seam opening closed up to the bottom of the zipper.

Turn the garment inside out and sew the top of the back of the hood together, using matching yarn and a tapestry needle.

Arm Ribbings

With the bag right side out, fold the long edge of the arm ribbing over the short edge, and pin in place. With a tapestry needle and yarn, sew the outside edges in place. You will be able to turn the rib back to expose baby's hand.

Finishing

Tie off and weave in any loose yarn ends on the inside of the bag.

Men's Picture Knit Sweater Vest

□ *Follow the instructions on page 10 with the following changes.*

□ *Materials*

1 pair size 2 needles
1 pair size 5 needles
1 set (4) size 2 double-pointed needles
3 stitch holders
1 tapestry needle
1 24″ size 2 round needle

□ *Back*

□ **Length.** Make length from beginning of rib to top border 2″ shorter. You will begin the top border pattern when the back measures 15 inches from the beginning of the rib.

□ **Underarm decrease.** Begin the underarm decrease by binding off 8 stitches at the beginning of each of the next 2 rows. Then bind off 1 stitch at the beginning of each of the next 16 rows. 85 (93) (101) stitches will remain.

□ **Shaping the shoulders.** When the work measures 9½ (10) (10½) inches straight up from the underarm decrease, the back is complete. Shape the shoulders in the following manner: Bind off 8 (9) (10) stitches at the beginning of each of the next 4 rows, then bind off 9 (11) (13) stitches at the beginning of each of the next 2 rows. Slip the remaining 35 stitches on a stitch holder for the back neck opening.

□ *Front*

□ **Length.** Start the top border pattern when the back measures 15 inches from the beginning of the rib.

□ **Underarm decrease.** Begin the underarm decrease by binding off 8 stitches at the beginning of each of the next 2 rows. Then bind off 1 stitch at the beginning of each of the next 16 rows. 85 (93) (101) stitches now remain.

□ **Making the V-neck.** When the top measures about 5 inches straight up from the beginning of the underarm decrease, work the V-neck in the following manner: Working from right (knit) side of front, knit 40 (44) (48) stitches and slip them on a stitch holder. Bind off the next 5 stitches, then work the last 40 (44) (48) stitches. Now you will work each side of the neck separately, starting with the left side. Bind off 1 stitch at the neck edge (every other row) until 25 (29) (33) stitches remain. Continue working the side until it measures 9½ (10) (10½) inches straight up from the underarm decrease (to match the back). Shape the shoulders as for the back of the vest. Repeat for the right side of the front.

Sew side seams and shoulder seams as per directions.

□ **Making the ribbing for the neck.** Using a size 2 24″ round needle, pick up and knit 112 stitches around the neck and work back and forth (as you would with straight needles) in a rib of k1, p1 for 7 rows. Bind off loosely. Now attach the rib edge, working from the wrong (purl) side of the sweater. Fold the right edge of the rib over the left edge. Using a tapestry needle, sew both edges and the front of the sweater (where you began the V by binding off 5 stitches) together.

□ **Making the armhole ribbings.** Using size 2 double-pointed needles, pick up and knit 80 (84) (88) stitches around the armhole, and work in a rib of k1, p1, for 7 rows. Bind off all stitches loosely.

Girl's Picture Knit Sweater Dress

□ *Follow pattern instructions on pages 13 - 15 with the following changes.*

□ **Yarn.** Purchase 1 additional skein of background color yarn.

□ **Size 2 (4) (6).** Add 8 (10) (10) additional inches to body in the length measurement only (from beginning of rib to beginning of top border pattern).

□ **Sizes 8 (10) (12).** Add 12 inches (all sizes) to body length measurement only (from beginning of rib to beginning of top border pattern).

Picture Knit Mittens

Since you will usually have enough yarn left over from a sweater project to make a pair of mittens, I have included mitten patterns for men's and women's sizes. The dog pattern shown here can be replaced with a design from your sweater if appropriate. A child's mitten does not have enough design space so a pattern is not included.

Men's mitten graph.

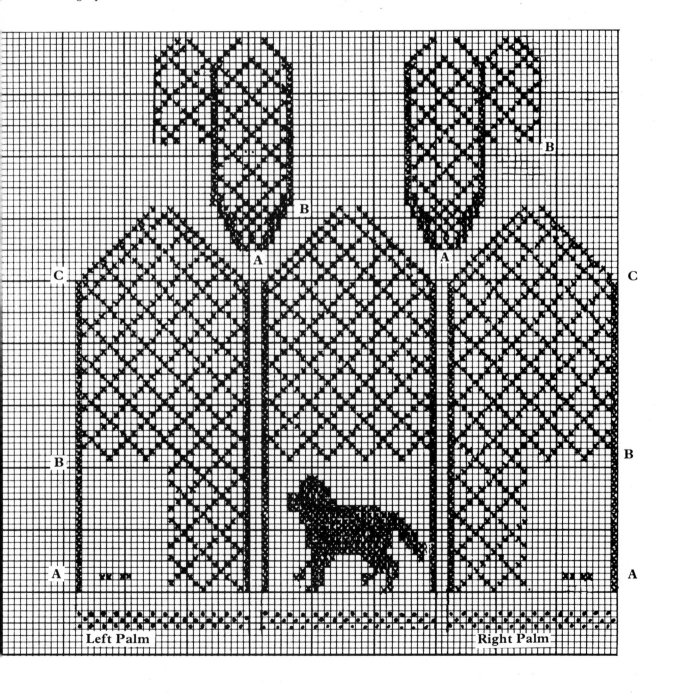

Men's Mitten Pattern

□ Gauge

6½ st per inch.

□ Materials

1 skein (3.5 oz.) Germantown knitting worsted for background.
1 small ball (about 1.5 oz.) Germantown knitting worsted for the picture pattern color.
1 very small ball (about .5 oz.) for border color.
1 set (4) size 2 double-pointed needles.

□ Stitches

Key to stitches: k = knit; p = purl.

Ribbing Stitch: For front and back pieces, k2, p2; for sleeves and neck, k1, p1.

Stockinette Stitch: Alternate rows of knit (right side) and purl (wrong side).

Using size 2 double-pointed needles, cast on 54 stitches and work around in a rib of k1, p1 until the work measures 3 inches from the beginning.
Then knit 1 row in a plain stockinette stitch and increase 2 stitches in this first row. There will be 56 stitches on the needles.

Begin following the diagram, working first the border, then the three plain rows, then the main pattern.
At point **A**, begin the lower part of the thumb (while making the hand) by increasing one stitch at each side of the thumb. In every other row, until there are 13 thumb stitches, knit the front and back of each of the outer pattern color stitches.
Continue following the diagram. At point **B**, take the 13 thumb stitches off the needle and place them on a safety pin. Continue knitting around the mitten. When you reach the thumb again, cast on 9 stitches for the back of the thumb area. Follow the diagram to point **C** (8 inches from **A** to **C**.).
At point **C**, begin decreasing by knitting 2 stitches together just inside the pattern color row on both the front and back of the mitten (4 stitches are decreased in every round of knitting). When there are 8 stitches left on the needles, pull both colors of yarn through the stitches. Break off the yarn (leave a length of about 6 inches), and fasten it firmly on the inside of the mitten.

□ Thumb

Now pick up the 13 stitches from the safety pin. Then pick up the 9 cast-on stitches at the back of the thumb, and 1 stitch on each side of the thumb opening — make 24 stitches in all. Follow the thumb diagram and make the thumb decreases as for the hand.
Be sure to reverse the palm for the other mitten.

Women's Mitten Pattern

□ Gauge

6½ st per inch.

□ Materials

1 skein (3.5 oz.) Germantown knitting worsted for background.
1 small ball (about 1.5 oz.) Germantown knitting worsted for the picture pattern color.
1 very small ball (about .5 oz.) for border color.
1 set (4) size 2 double-pointed needles.

□ Stitches

Key to stitches: k = knit; p = purl.

Ribbing Stitch: For front and back pieces, k2, p2; for sleeves and neck, k1, p1.

Stockinette Stitch: Alternate rows of knit (right side) and purl (wrong side).

Using size 2 double-pointed needles, cast on 48 stitches and work around in a rib of k1, p1 until the work measures 3 inches from the beginning.
Then knit 1 row in a plain stockinette stitch and increase 2 stitches in this first row. There will be 50 stitches on the needles.

Begin following the diagram, working first the border, then the three plain rows, then the main pattern.
At point **A**, begin the lower part of the thumb (while making the hand) by increasing one stitch at each side of the thumb. In every other row, knit the front and back of each of the outer pattern color stitches until there are 11 thumb stitches.
Continue following the diagram. At point **B**, take the 11 thumb stitches off the needle and place them on a safety pin. Continue knitting around the mitten. When you reach the thumb again, cast on 7 stitches for the back of the thumb area. Follow the diagram to point **C**. (7 inches from **A** to **C**.)
At point **C**, begin decreasing by knitting 2 stitches together just inside the pattern color row on both the front and back of the mitten (4 stitches are decreased in every round of knitting). When there are 8 stitches left on the needles, pull both colors of yarn through the stitches. Break off the yarn (leave a length of about 6 inches), and fasten it firmly on the inside of the mitten.

□ Thumb

Now pick up the 11 stitches from the safety pin. Then pick up the 7 cast-on stitches at the back of the thumb, and 1 stitch on each side of the thumb opening — making 20 stitches in all. Follow the thumb diagram and make the thumb decreases as for the hand.
Be sure to reverse the palm for the other mitten.

Women's mitten graph.

Left Palm   Right Palm

9.
Extra Patterns

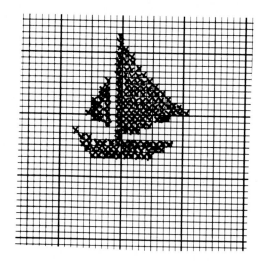

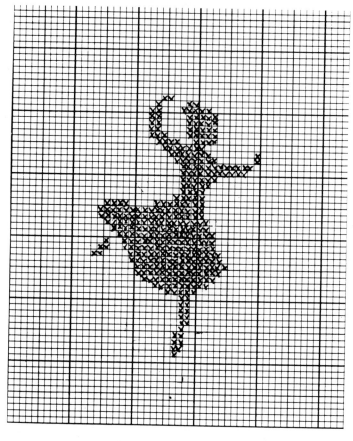

*Above and Right:
These nautical
designs would be very
good for a cotton
children's sweater.*

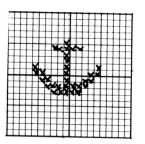

*Above:
Any girl would love a sweater with these beautiful ballerinas
dancing across the top. Use two repeats for a girl's size
sweater.*

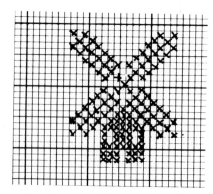

*Above:
Windmill.*

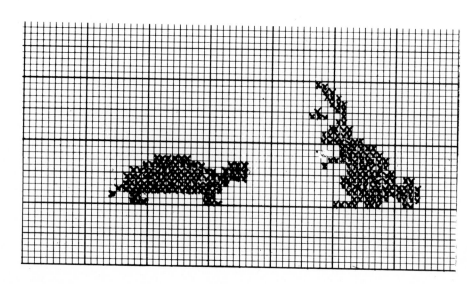

*Left:
The Tortoise and the Hare.*

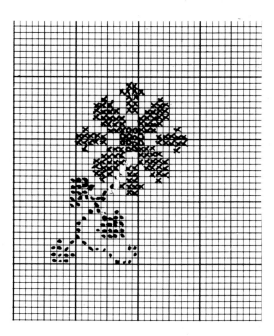

Left and Below:
Combine penguins and pine trees in a warm winter sweater. Embroider one stitch of red for the penguin's eye.

Above:
Use as a repeating design for women's and girl's sweaters.

Right:
Use as a lovely accent or border element.

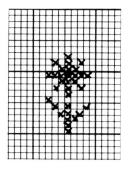

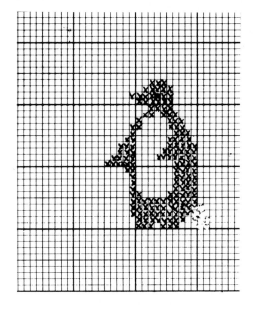

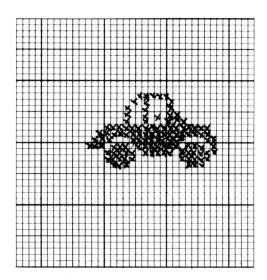

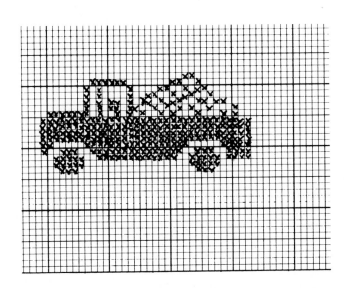

Above and Right:
Use separately or combine these truck and car patterns for the men in your life.

Dachshund.

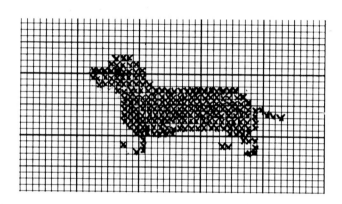

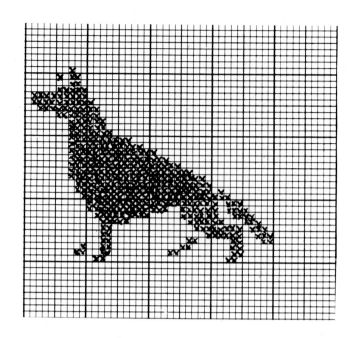

German Shepherd.

Schnauzer.

Right:
Mix and match
these border
patterns to
personalize your
designs.

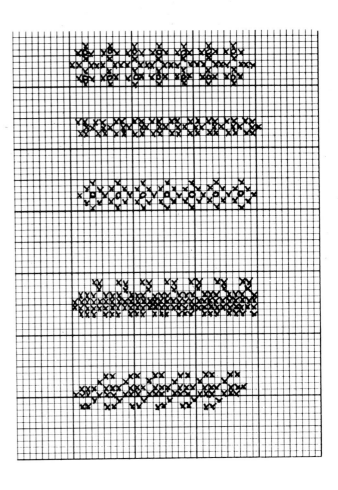

Use these knitting alphabets to spell out names on your
sweaters, or make monograms.

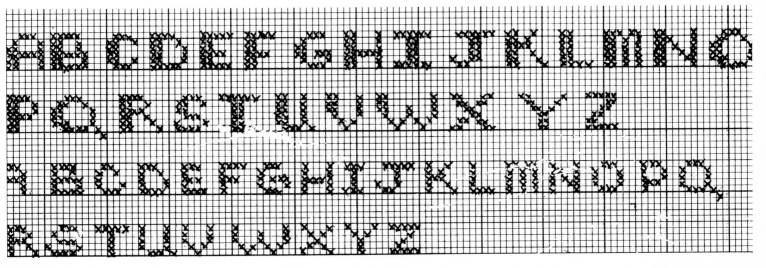

□ *Machine Knitting Conversion Chart*

Sweater Name _____ **Page #** _____

Gauge _____ at tension dial setting _____

Cast on _____ st. for size _____

_____ rows/inch

_____ rows from **A** to **B** (beginning of bottom border to beginning of top border)

_____ rows from **B** to **C** (for top border)

_____ rows from **C** to **D** (from end of top border to bind-off)

_____ rows from **A** to **B** (for arm)

□ *Machine Knitting Conversion Chart*

Sweater Name _____ **Page #** _____

Gauge _____ at tension dial setting _____

Cast on _____ st. for size _____

_____ rows/inch

_____ rows from **A** to **B** (beginning of bottom border to beginning of top border)

_____ rows from **B** to **C** (for top border)

_____ rows from **C** to **D** (from end of top border to bind-off)

_____ rows from **A** to **B** (for arm)

□ *Machine Knitting Conversion Chart*

Sweater Name _____ **Page #** _____

Gauge _____ at tension dial setting _____

Cast on _____ st. for size _____

_____ rows/inch

_____ rows from **A** to **B** (beginning of bottom border to beginning of top border)

_____ rows from **B** to **C** (for top border)

_____ rows from **C** to **D** (from end of top border to bind-off)

_____ rows from **A** to **B** (for arm)

□ *Machine Knitting Conversion Chart*

Sweater Name _____ **Page #** _____

Gauge _____ at tension dial setting _____

Cast on _____ st. for size _____

_____ rows/inch

_____ rows from **A** to **B** (beginning of bottom border to beginning of top border)

_____ rows from **B** to **C** (for top border)

_____ rows from **C** to **D** (from end of top border to bind-off)

_____ rows from **A** to **B** (for arm)

□ *Machine Knitting Conversion Chart*

Sweater Name _____ **Page #** _____

Gauge _____ at tension dial setting _____

Cast on _____ st. for size _____

_____ rows/inch

_____ rows from **A** to **B** (beginning of bottom border to beginning of top border)

_____ rows from **B** to **C** (for top border)

_____ rows from **C** to **D** (from end of top border to bind-off)

_____ rows from **A** to **B** (for arm)

□ *Machine Knitting Conversion Chart*

Sweater Name _____ **Page #** _____

Gauge _____ at tension dial setting _____

Cast on _____ st. for size _____

_____ rows/inch

_____ rows from **A** to **B** (beginning of bottom border to beginning of top border)

_____ rows from **B** to **C** (for top border)

_____ rows from **C** to **D** (from end of top border to bind-off)

_____ rows from **A** to **B** (for arm)

□ *Machine Knitting Conversion Chart*

Sweater Name _____ **Page #** _____

Gauge _____ at tension dial setting _____

Cast on _____ st. for size _____

_____ rows/inch

_____ rows from **A** to **B** (beginning of bottom border to beginning of top border)

_____ rows from **B** to **C** (for top border)

_____ rows from **C** to **D** (from end of top border to bind-off)

_____ rows from **A** to **B** (for arm)

□ *Machine Knitting Conversion Chart*

Sweater Name _____ **Page #** _____

Gauge _____ at tension dial setting _____

Cast on _____ st. for size _____

_____ rows/inch

_____ rows from **A** to **B** (beginning of bottom border to beginning of top border)

_____ rows from **B** to **C** (for top border)

_____ rows from **C** to **D** (from end of top border to bind-off)

_____ rows from **A** to **B** (for arm)

☐ *Machine Knitting Conversion Chart*

Sweater Name _____ **Page #** _____

Gauge _____ at tension dial setting _____

Cast on _____ st. for size _____

_____ rows/inch

_____ rows from **A** to **B** (beginning of bottom border to beginning of top border)

_____ rows from **B** to **C** (for top border)

_____ rows from **C** to **D** (from end of top border to bind-off)

_____ rows from **A** to **B** (for arm)

☐ *Machine Knitting Conversion Chart*

Sweater Name _____ **Page #** _____

Gauge _____ at tension dial setting _____

Cast on _____ st. for size _____

_____ rows/inch

_____ rows from **A** to **B** (beginning of bottom border to beginning of top border)

_____ rows from **B** to **C** (for top border)

_____ rows from **C** to **D** (from end of top border to bind-off)

_____ rows from **A** to **B** (for arm)

☐ *Machine Knitting Conversion Chart*

Sweater Name _____ **Page #** _____

Gauge _____ at tension dial setting _____

Cast on _____ st. for size _____

_____ rows/inch

_____ rows from **A** to **B** (beginning of bottom border to beginning of top border)

_____ rows from **B** to **C** (for top border)

_____ rows from **C** to **D** (from end of top border to bind-off)

_____ rows from **A** to **B** (for arm)

☐ *Machine Knitting Conversion Chart*

Sweater Name _____ **Page #** _____

Gauge _____ at tension dial setting _____

Cast on _____ st. for size _____

_____ rows/inch

_____ rows from **A** to **B** (beginning of bottom border to beginning of top border)

_____ rows from **B** to **C** (for top border)

_____ rows from **C** to **D** (from end of top border to bind-off)

_____ rows from **A** to **B** (for arm)

☐ *Machine Knitting Conversion Chart*

Sweater Name _____ **Page #** _____

Gauge _____ at tension dial setting _____

Cast on _____ st. for size _____

_____ rows/inch

_____ rows from **A** to **B** (beginning of bottom border to beginning of top border)

_____ rows from **B** to **C** (for top border)

_____ rows from **C** to **D** (from end of top border to bind-off)

_____ rows from **A** to **B** (for arm)

☐ *Machine Knitting Conversion Chart*

Sweater Name _____ **Page #** _____

Gauge _____ at tension dial setting _____

Cast on _____ st. for size _____

_____ rows/inch

_____ rows from **A** to **B** (beginning of bottom border to beginning of top border)

_____ rows from **B** to **C** (for top border)

_____ rows from **C** to **D** (from end of top border to bind-off)

_____ rows from **A** to **B** (for arm)

☐ *Machine Knitting Conversion Chart*

Sweater Name _____ **Page #** _____

Gauge _____ at tension dial setting _____

Cast on _____ st. for size _____

_____ rows/inch

_____ rows from **A** to **B** (beginning of bottom border to beginning of top border)

_____ rows from **B** to **C** (for top border)

_____ rows from **C** to **D** (from end of top border to bind-off)

_____ rows from **A** to **B** (for arm)

☐ *Machine Knitting Conversion Charts*

Sweater Name _____ **Page #** _____

Gauge _____ at tension dial setting _____

Cast on _____ st. for size _____

_____ rows/inch

_____ rows from **A** to **B** (beginning of bottom border to beginning of top border)

_____ rows from **B** to **C** (for top border)

_____ rows from **C** to **D** (from end of top border to bind-off)

_____ rows from **A** to **B** (for arm)

☐ *Machine Knitting Conversion Chart*

Sweater Name _____ **Page #** _____

Gauge _____ at tension dial setting _____

Cast on _____ st. for size _____

_____ rows/inch

_____ rows from **A** to **B** (beginning of bottom border to beginning of top border)

_____ rows from **B** to **C** (for top border)

_____ rows from **C** to **D** (from end of top border to bind-off)

_____ rows from **A** to **B** (for arm)

☐ *Machine Knitting Conversion Chart*

Sweater Name _____ **Page #** _____

Gauge _____ at tension dial setting _____

Cast on _____ st. for size _____

_____ rows/inch

_____ rows from **A** to **B** (beginning of bottom border to beginning of top border)

_____ rows from **B** to **C** (for top border)

_____ rows from **C** to **D** (from end of top border to bind-off)

_____ rows from **A** to **B** (for arm)

☐ *Machine Knitting Conversion Chart*

Sweater Name _____ **Page #** _____

Gauge _____ at tension dial setting _____

Cast on _____ st. for size _____

_____ rows/inch

_____ rows from **A** to **B** (beginning of bottom border to beginning of top border)

_____ rows from **B** to **C** (for top border)

_____ rows from **C** to **D** (from end of top border to bind-off)

_____ rows from **A** to **B** (for arm)

☐ *Machine Knitting Conversion Chart*

Sweater Name _____ **Page #** _____

Gauge _____ at tension dial setting _____

Cast on _____ st. for size _____

_____ rows/inch

_____ rows from **A** to **B** (beginning of bottom border to beginning of top border)

_____ rows from **B** to **C** (for top border)

_____ rows from **C** to **D** (from end of top border to bind-off)

_____ rows from **A** to **B** (for arm)

☐ *Machine Knitting Conversion Chart*

Sweater Name _____ **Page #** _____

Gauge _____ at tension dial setting _____

Cast on _____ st. for size _____

_____ rows/inch

_____ rows from **A** to **B** (beginning of bottom border to beginning of top border)

_____ rows from **B** to **C** (for top border)

_____ rows from **C** to **D** (from end of top border to bind-off)

_____ rows from **A** to **B** (for arm)

☐ *Machine Knitting Conversion Chart*

Sweater Name _____ **Page #** _____

Gauge _____ at tension dial setting _____

Cast on _____ st. for size _____

_____ rows/inch

_____ rows from **A** to **B** (beginning of bottom border to beginning of top border)

_____ rows from **B** to **C** (for top border)

_____ rows from **C** to **D** (from end of top border to bind-off)

_____ rows from **A** to **B** (for arm)

❏ *Machine Knitting Conversion Chart*

Sweater Name _____ Page # _____

Gauge _____ at tension dial setting _____

Cast on _____ st. for size _____

_____ rows/inch

_____ rows from **A** to **B** (beginning of bottom border to beginning of top border)

_____ rows from **B** to **C** (for top border)

_____ rows from **C** to **D** (from end of top border to bind-off)

_____ rows from **A** to **B** (for arm)

❏ *Machine Knitting Conversion Chart*

Sweater Name _____ Page # _____

Gauge _____ at tension dial setting _____

Cast on _____ st. for size _____

_____ rows/inch

_____ rows from **A** to **B** (beginning of bottom border to beginning of top border)

_____ rows from **B** to **C** (for top border)

_____ rows from **C** to **D** (from end of top border to bind-off)

_____ rows from **A** to **B** (for arm)

❏ *Machine Knitting Conversion Chart*

Sweater Name _____ Page # _____

Gauge _____ at tension dial setting _____

Cast on _____ st. for size _____

_____ rows/inch

_____ rows from **A** to **B** (beginning of bottom border to beginning of top border)

_____ rows from **B** to **C** (for top border)

_____ rows from **C** to **D** (from end of top border to bind-off)

_____ rows from **A** to **B** (for arm)

❏ *Machine Knitting Conversion Chart*

Sweater Name _____ Page # _____

Gauge _____ at tension dial setting _____

Cast on _____ st. for size _____

_____ rows/inch

_____ rows from **A** to **B** (beginning of bottom border to beginning of top border)

_____ rows from **B** to **C** (for top border)

_____ rows from **C** to **D** (from end of top border to bind-off)

_____ rows from **A** to **B** (for arm)

❏ *Machine Knitting Conversion Chart*

Sweater Name _____ Page # _____

Gauge _____ at tension dial setting _____

Cast on _____ st. for size _____

_____ rows/inch

_____ rows from **A** to **B** (beginning of bottom border to beginning of top border)

_____ rows from **B** to **C** (for top border)

_____ rows from **C** to **D** (from end of top border to bind-off)

_____ rows from **A** to **B** (for arm)

❏ *Machine Knitting Conversion Chart*

Sweater Name _____ Page # _____

Gauge _____ at tension dial setting _____

Cast on _____ st. for size _____

_____ rows/inch

_____ rows from **A** to **B** (beginning of bottom border to beginning of top border)

_____ rows from **B** to **C** (for top border)

_____ rows from **C** to **D** (from end of top border to bind-off)

_____ rows from **A** to **B** (for arm)

Index

Bibliography

Brown, Theodore L., and Curtis LeMay, Jr.
Chemistry the Central Science. Englewood Cliffs,
New Jersey: Prentice-Hall, Inc., 1977.

Carroll, Alice.
*Knitting and Crocheting Your Own Fashions of The
Forties.* New York: Dover Publications, Inc., 1973.

Carter, Valerie.
Machine Knits. Asheville, North Carolina: Lark
Books, 1986.

Gioello, Debbie Ann, and Beverly Berke.
Figure Types and Size Ranges. New York:
Fairchild Publications, 1979.

Gottfridsson, Inger, and Ingrid Gottfridsson.
The Mitten Book. Asheville, North Carolina: Lark
Books, 1987.

Lewis, Susanna, and Julia Weissman.
A Machine Knitter's Guide to Creating Fabrics.
Asheville, North Carolina: Lark Books, 1987.

Palmer, Pati and Susan Pletsch.
Mother Pletsch's Painless Sewing. Portland, Oregon:
Pati Palmer and Susan Pletsch, 1975.

The Vogue Sewing Book. Rev. ed.
New York: Butterick Publishing — Div. of
American Can Company, 1975.